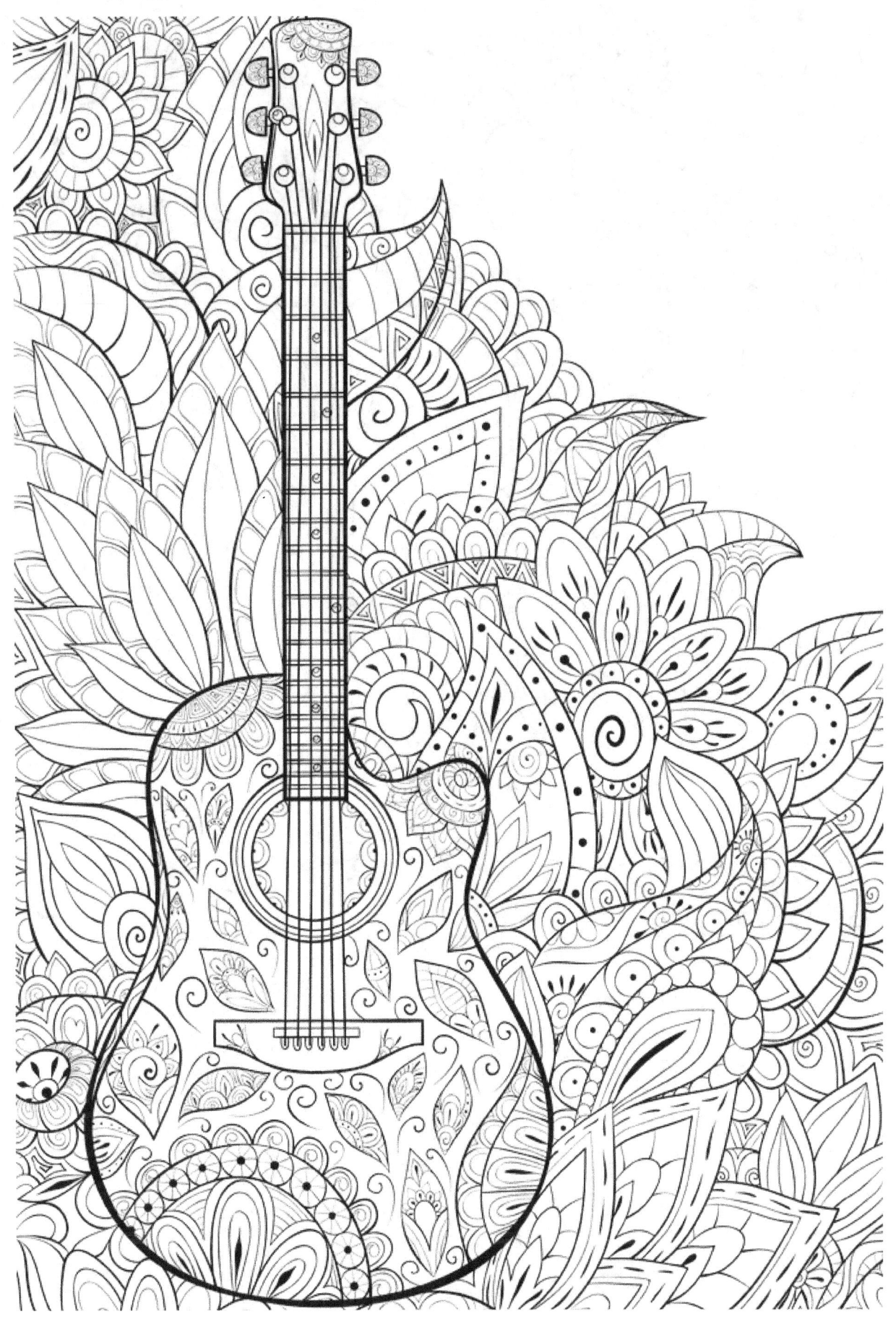

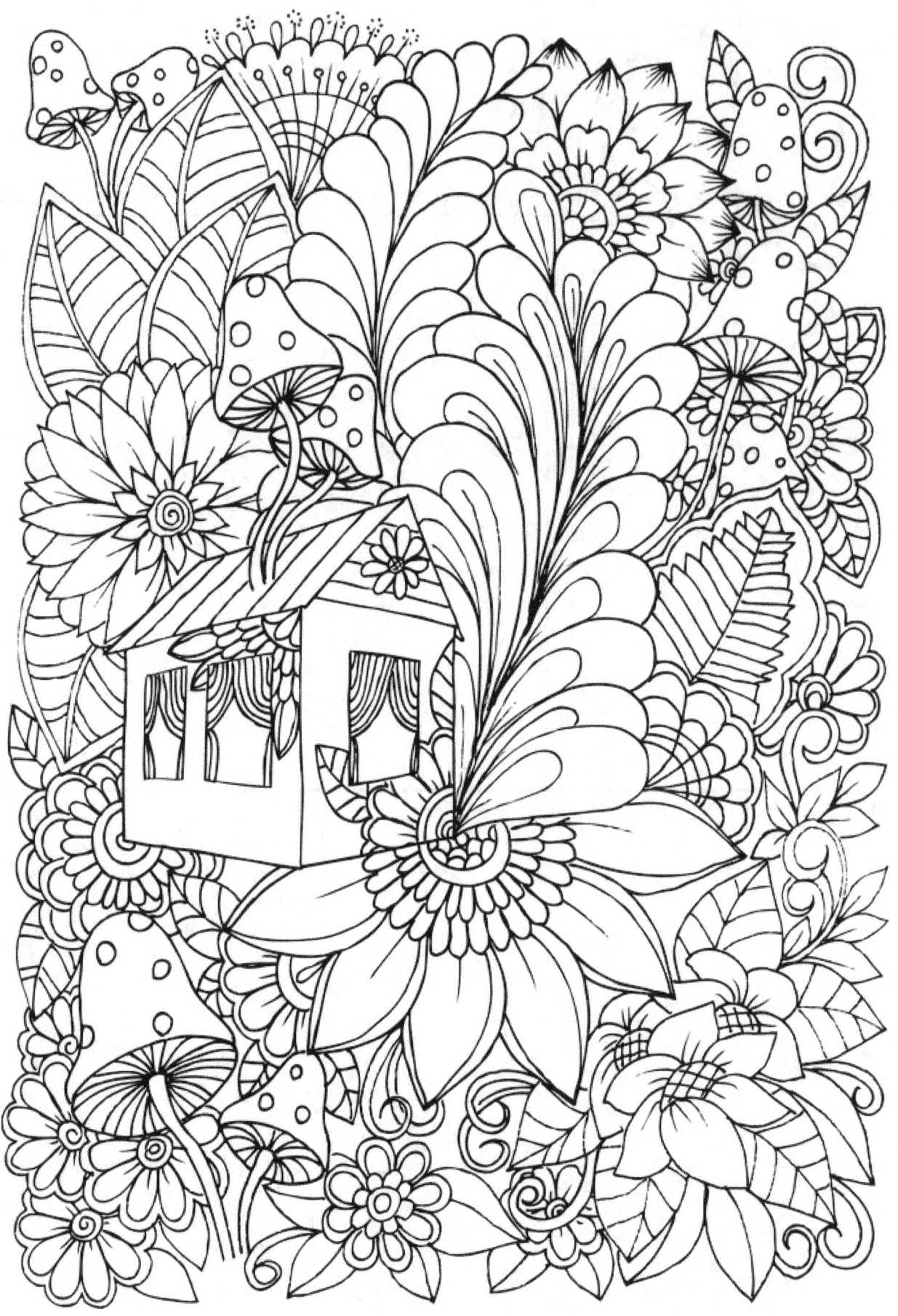

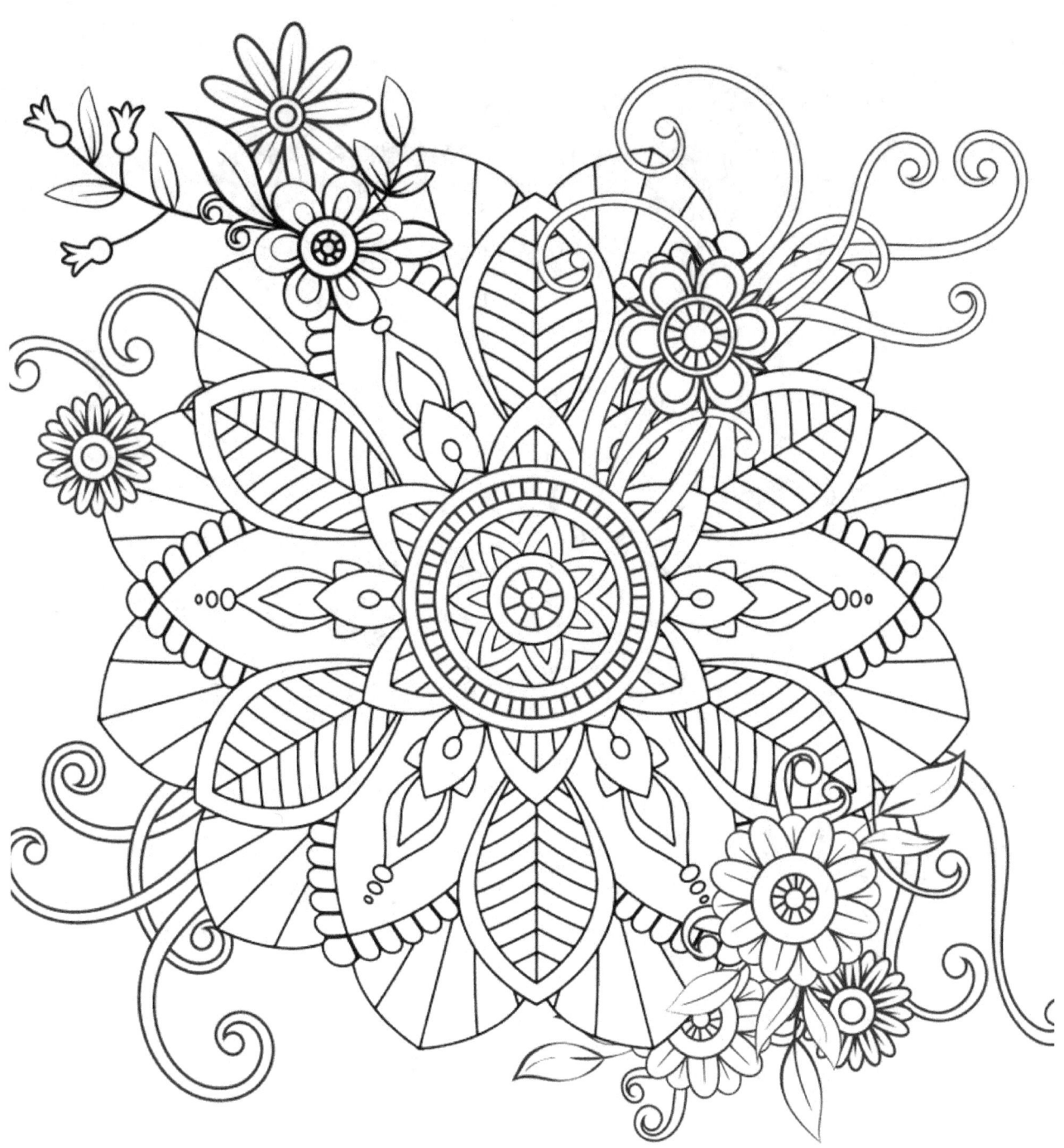

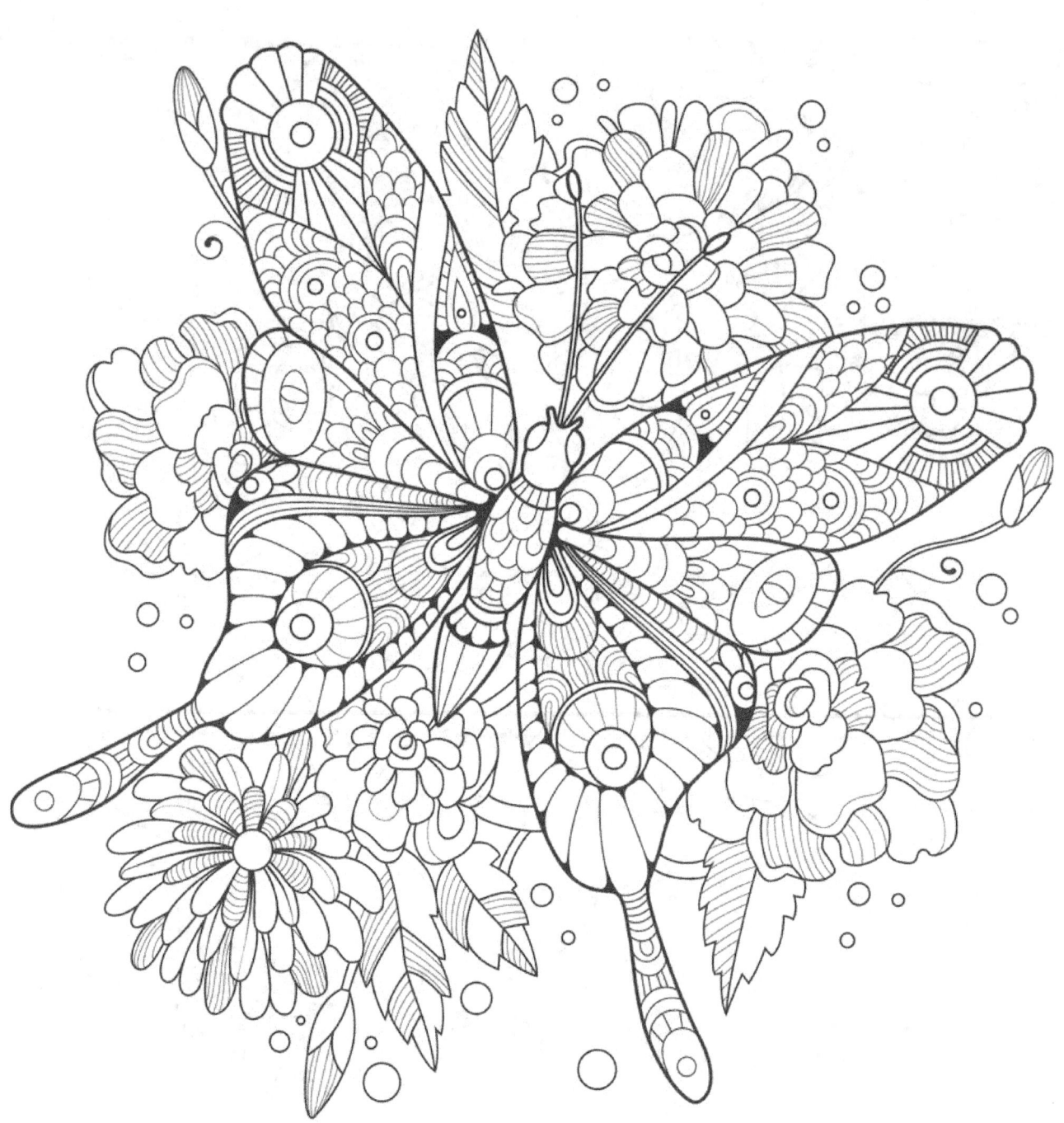

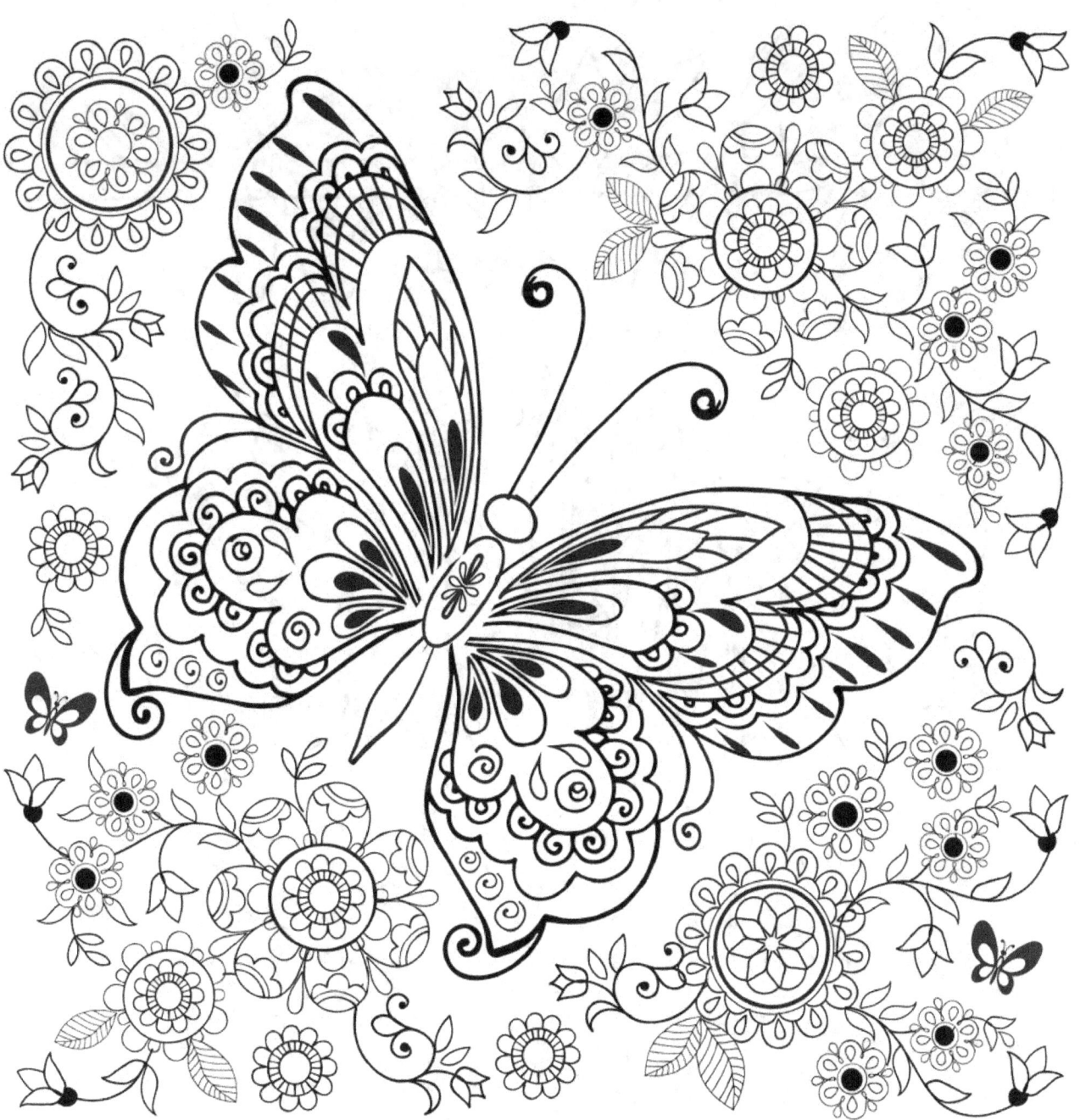

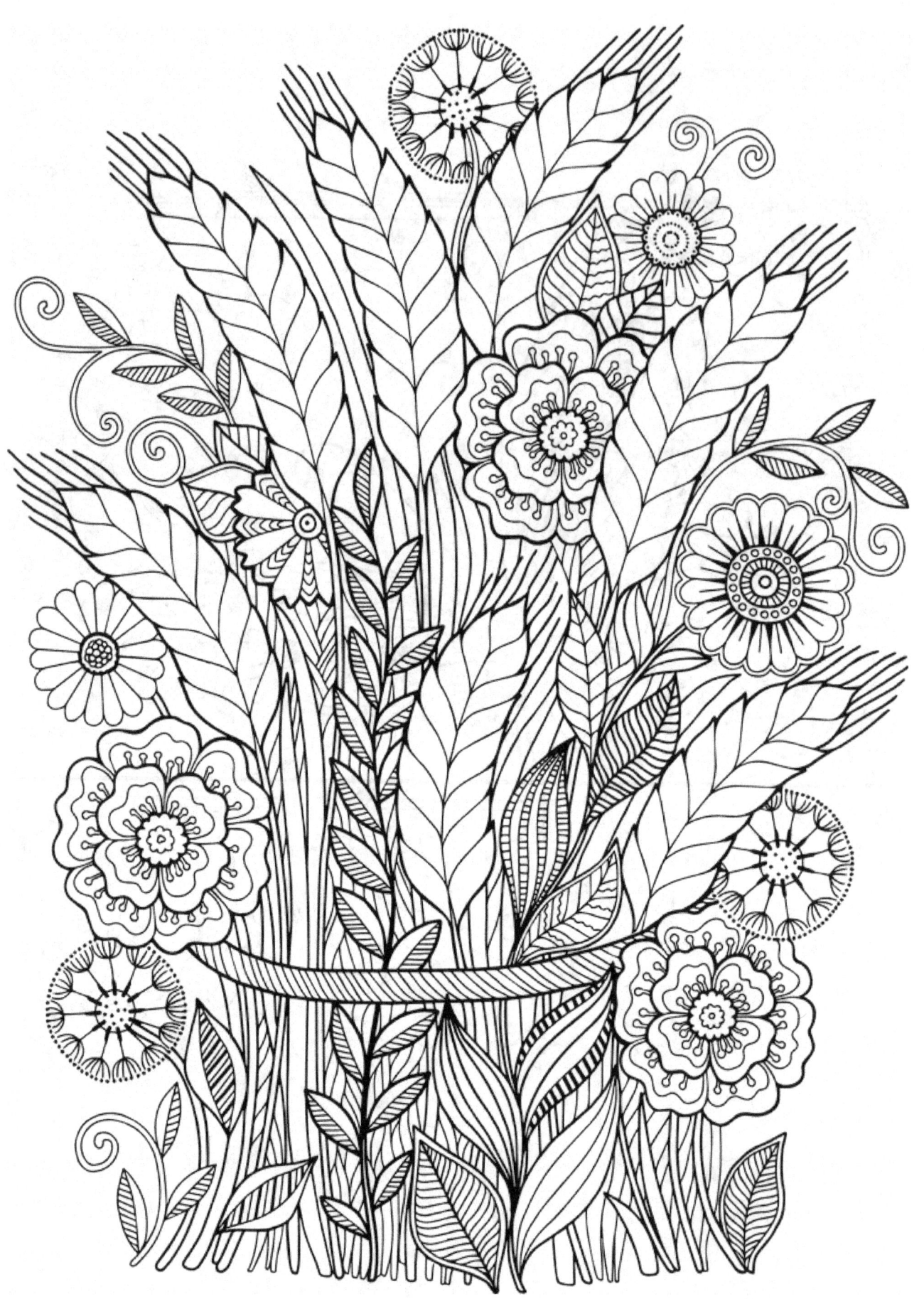

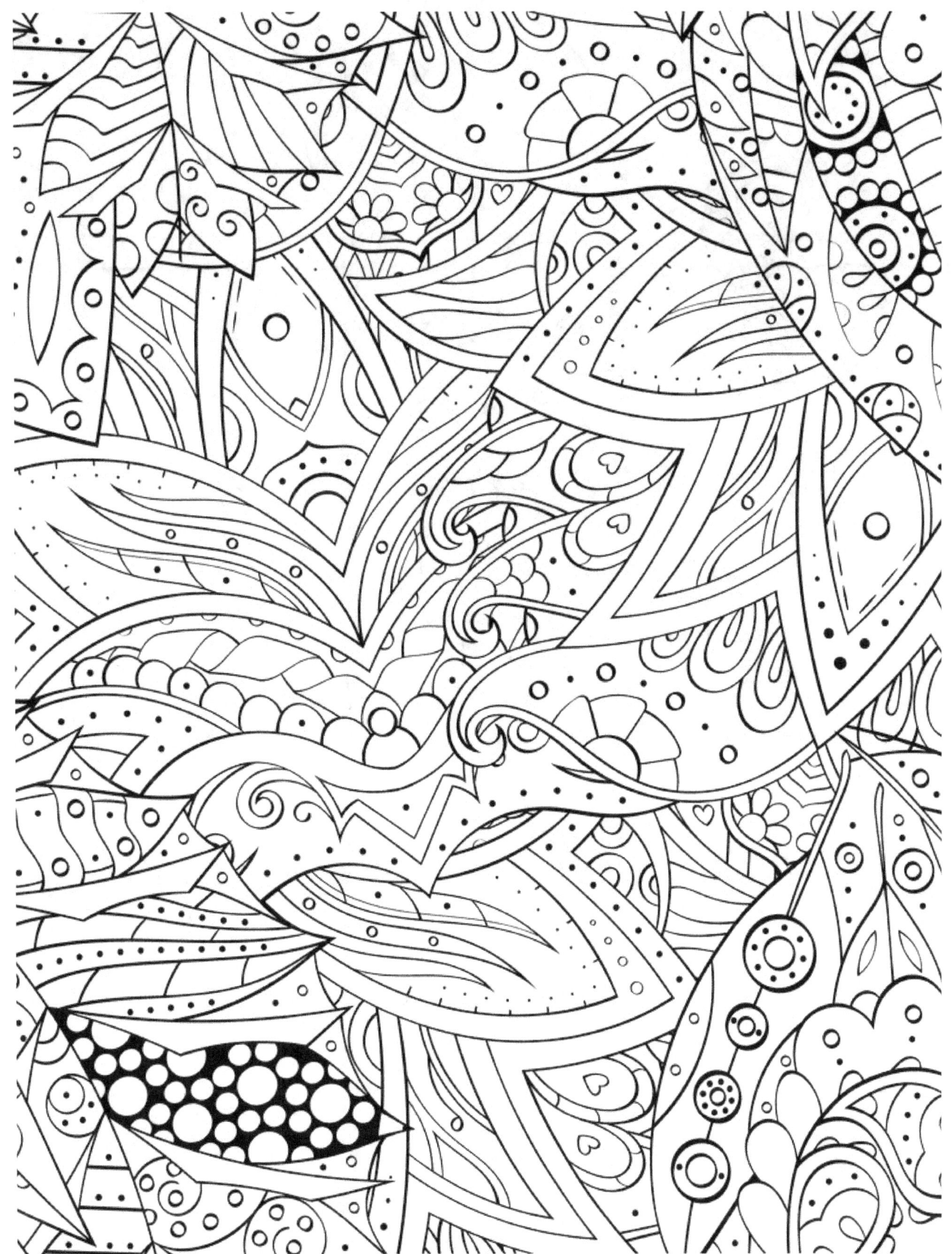

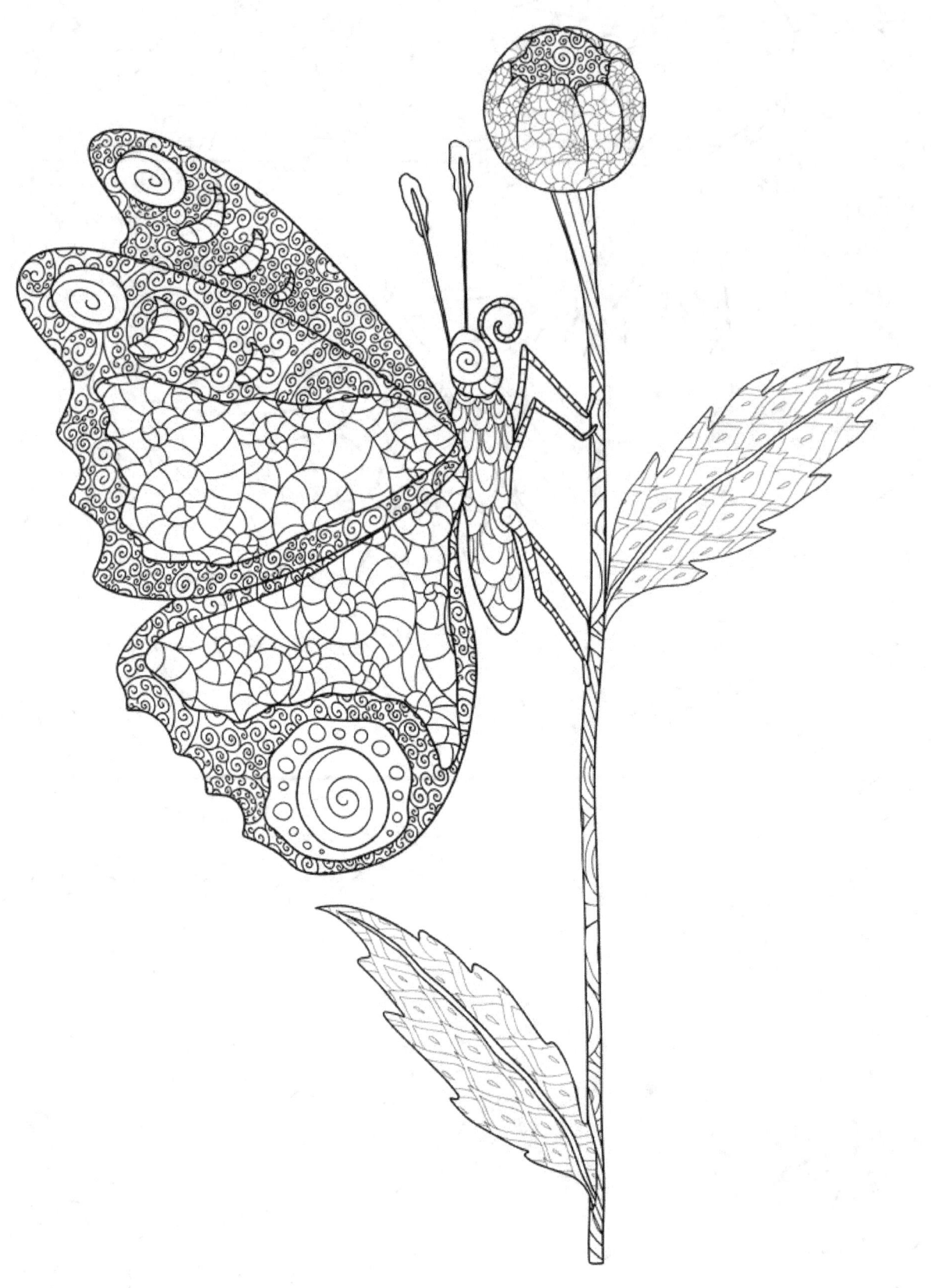

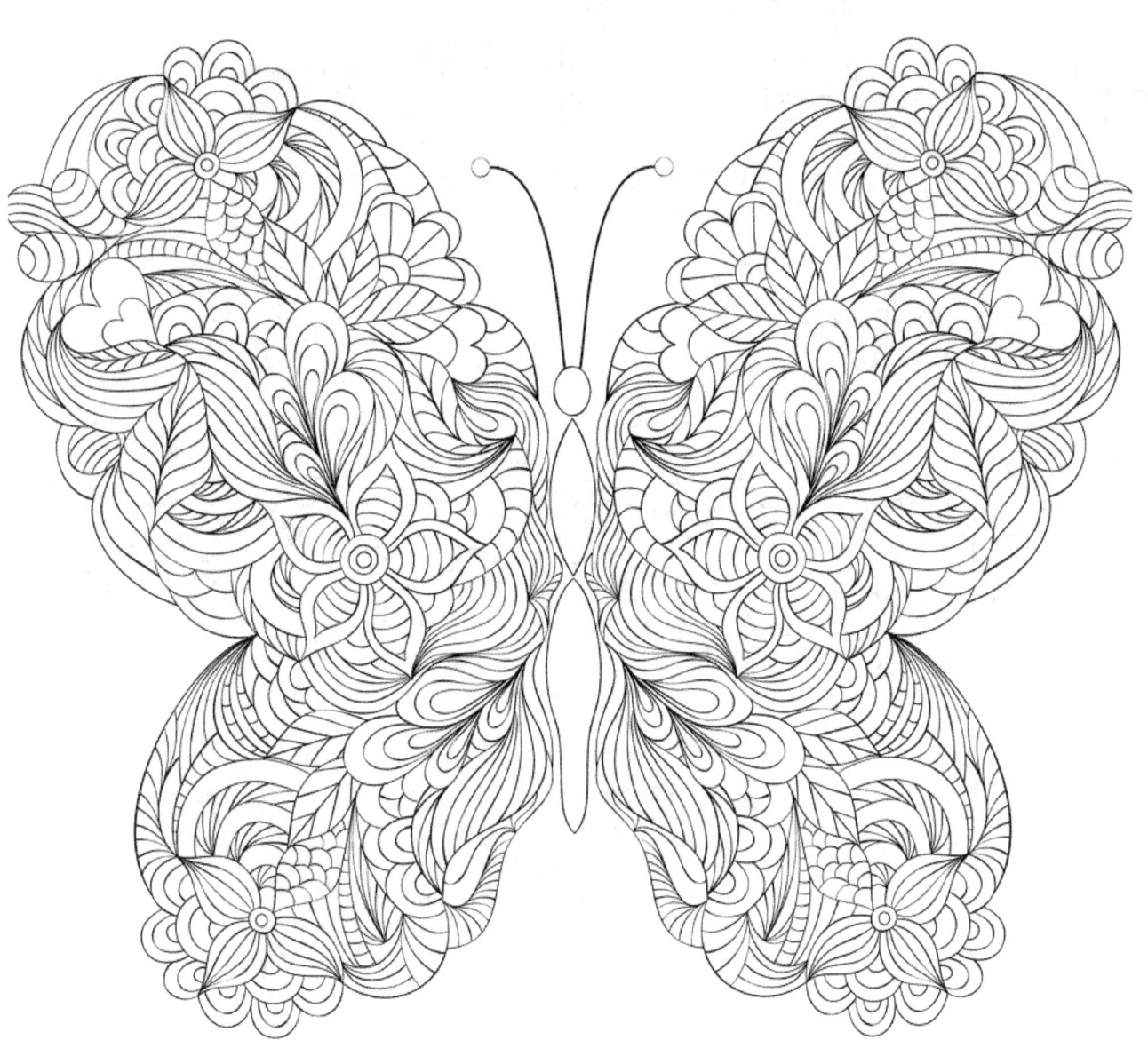

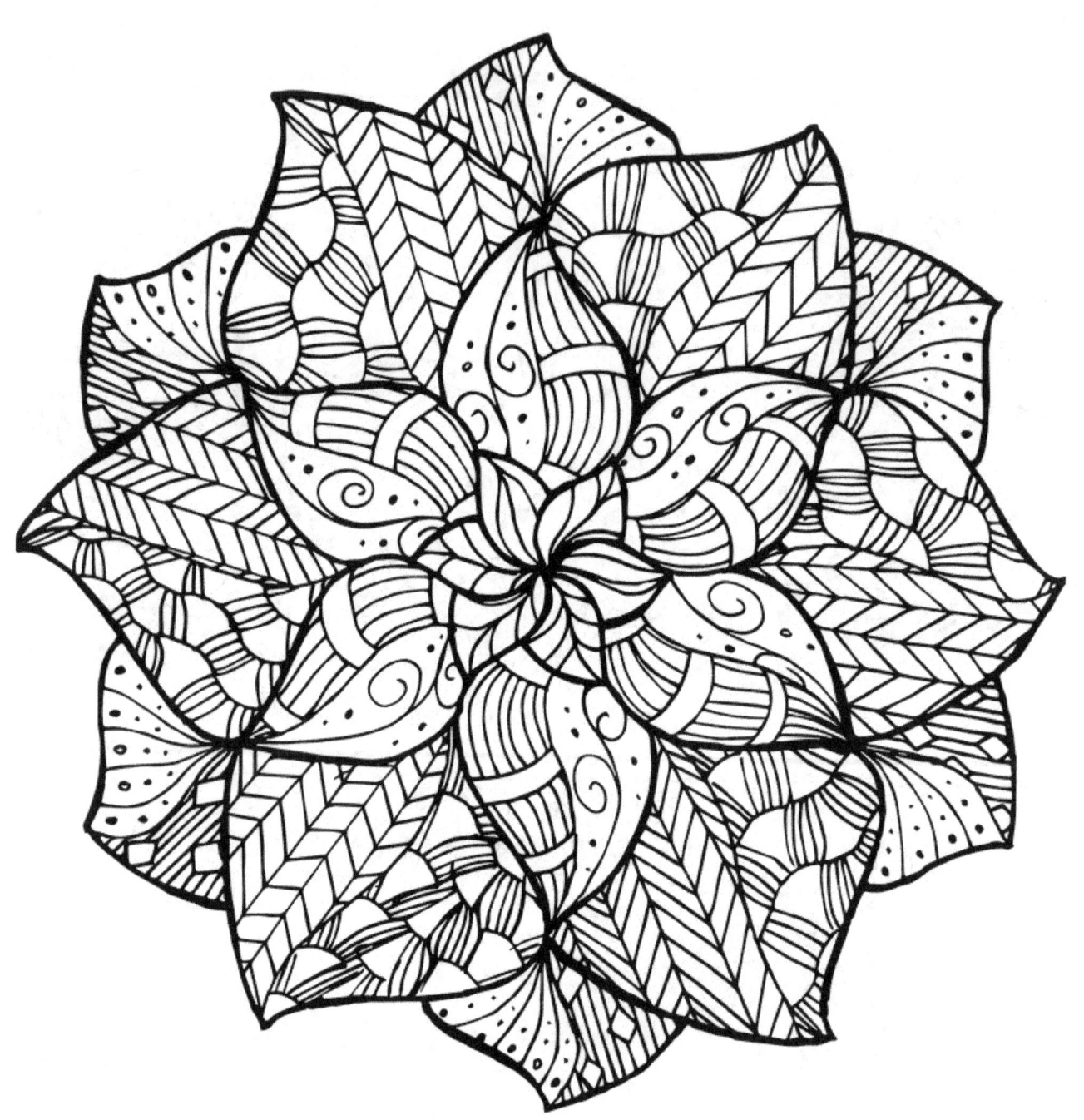

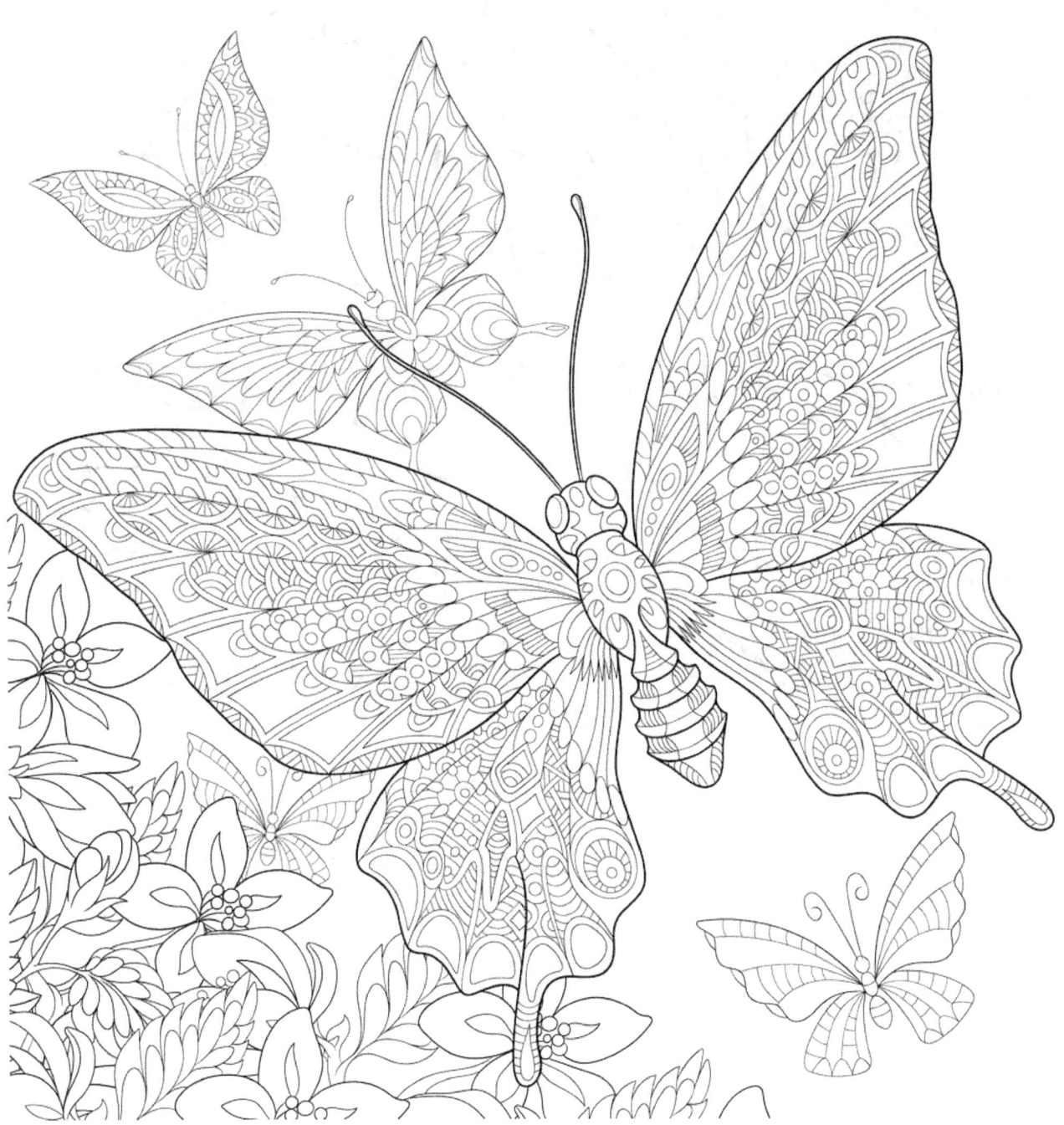

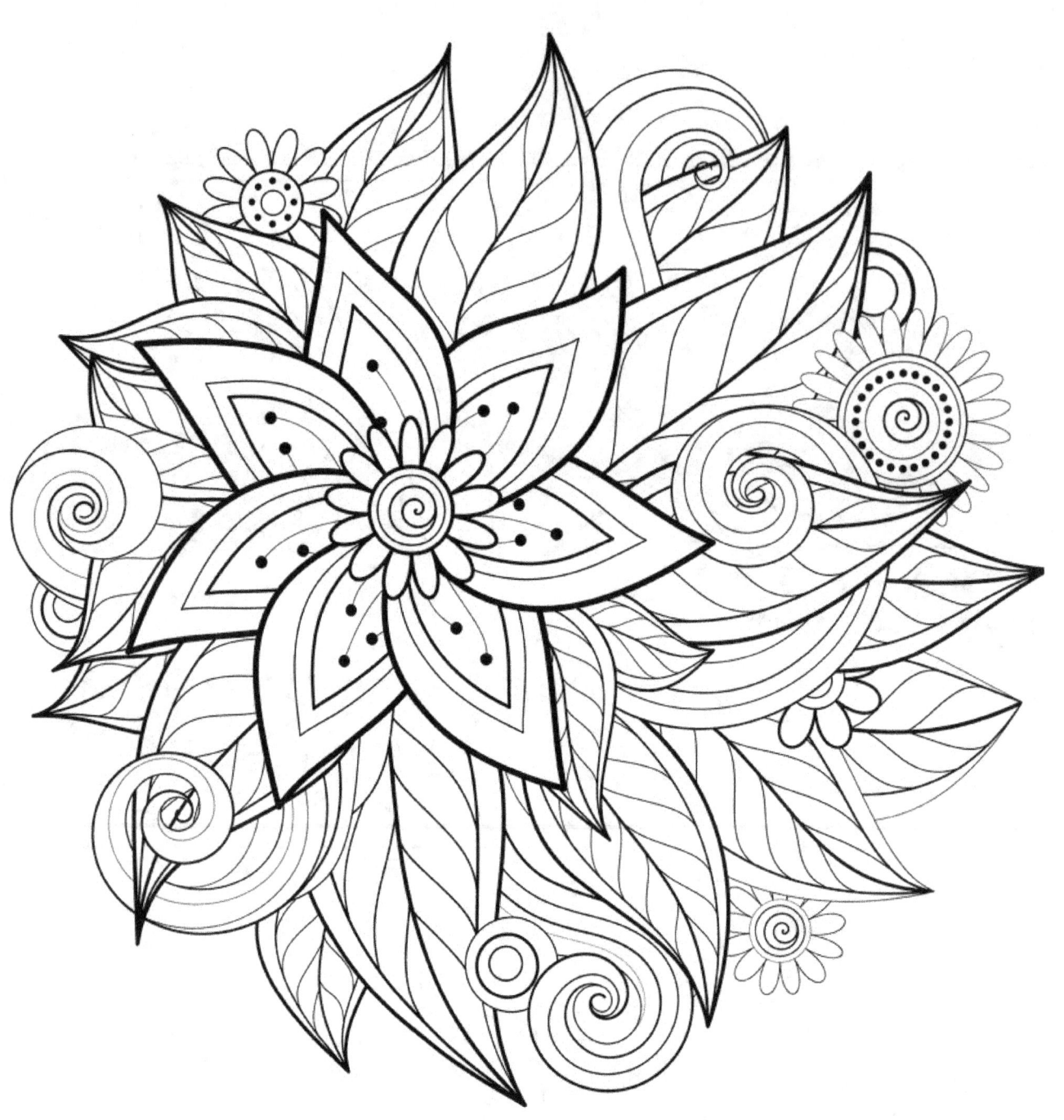

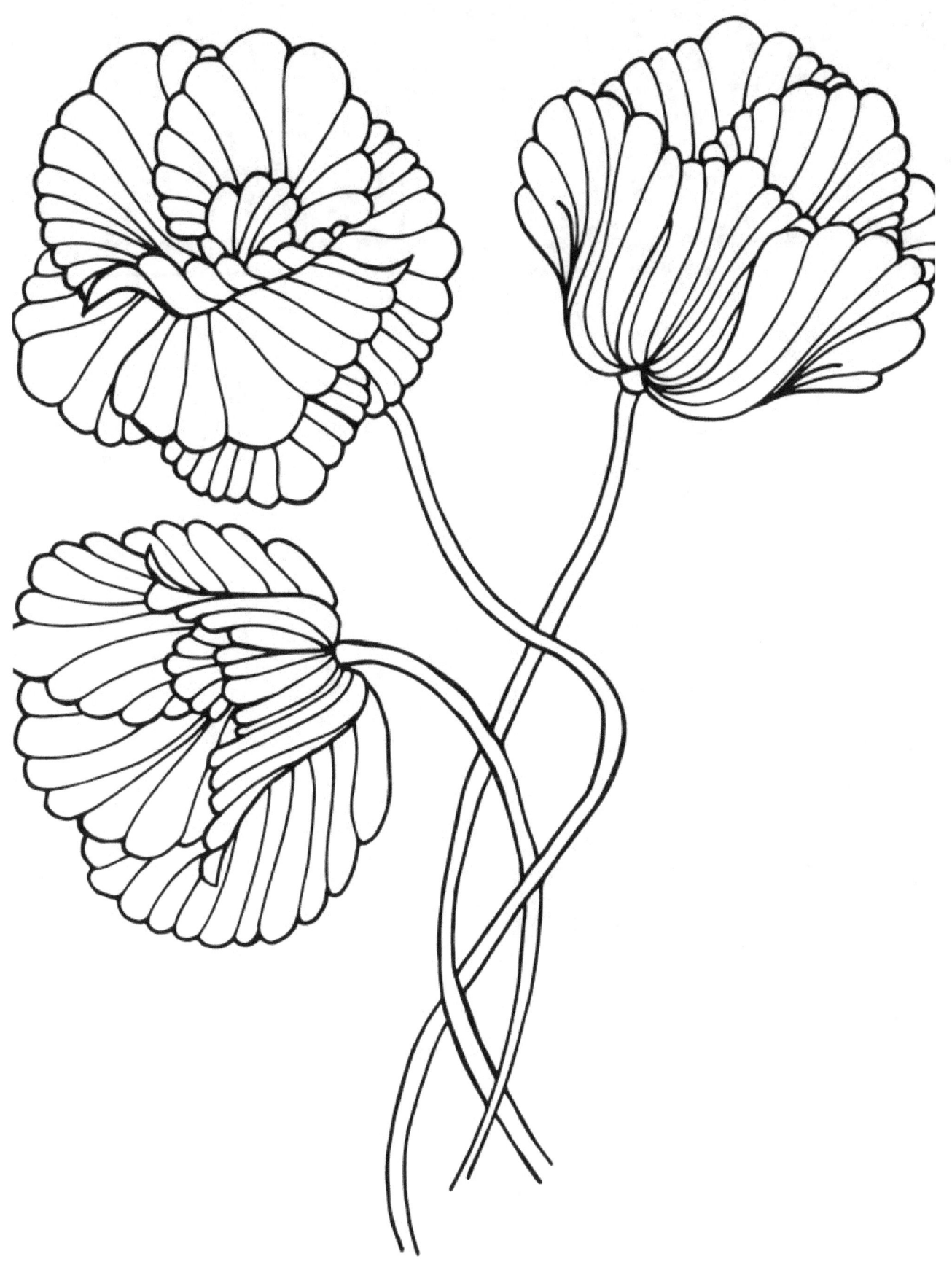

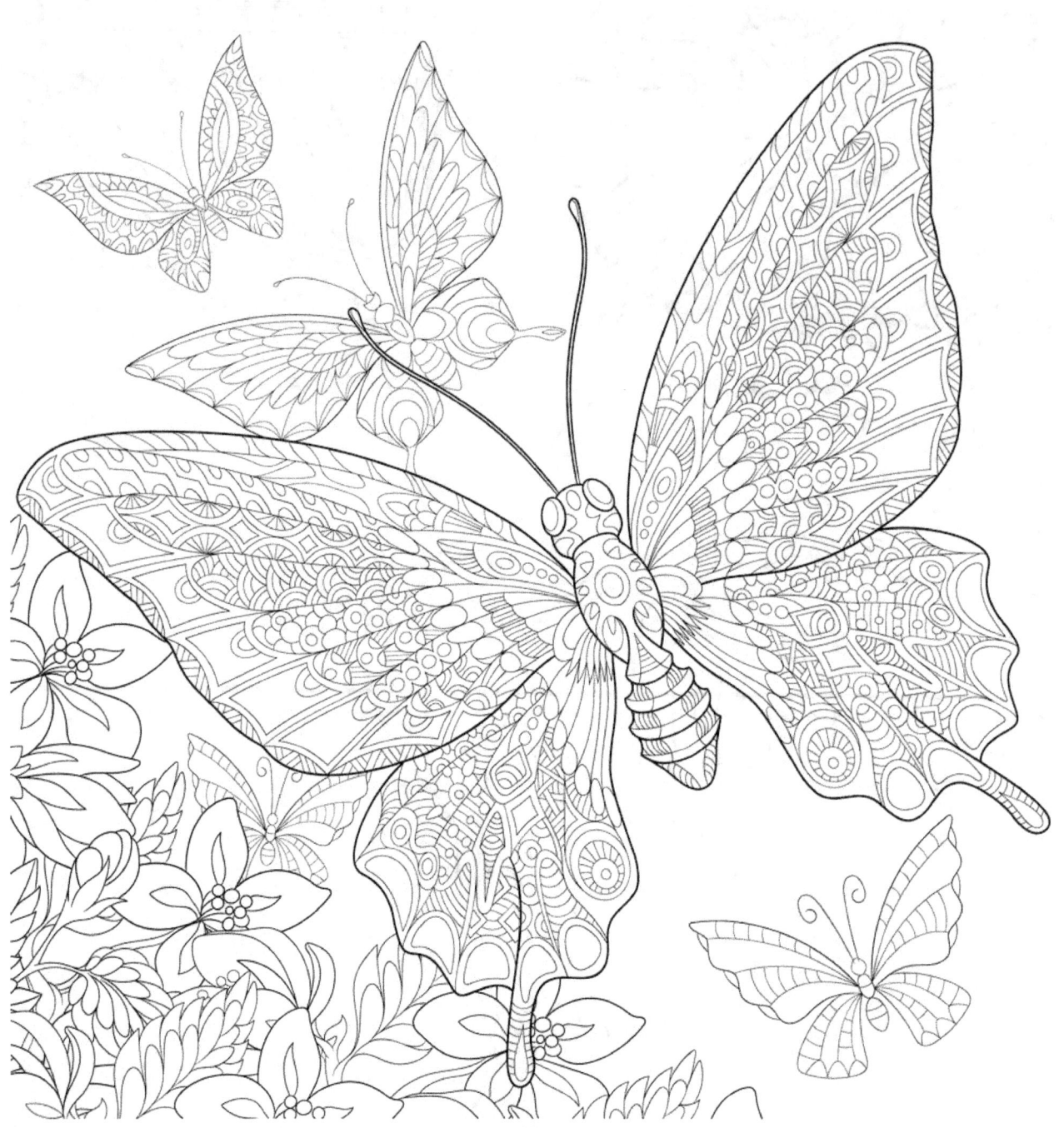

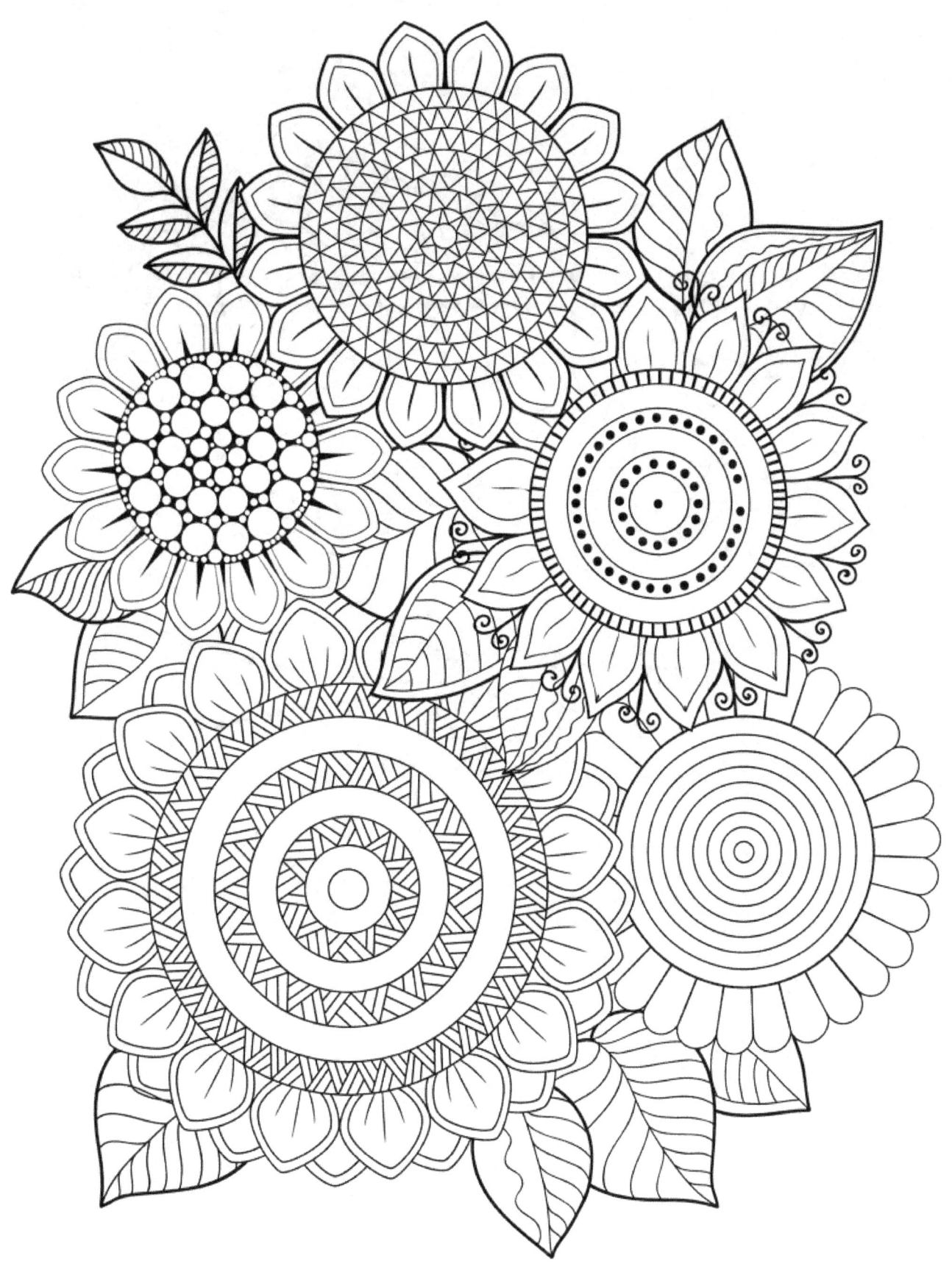

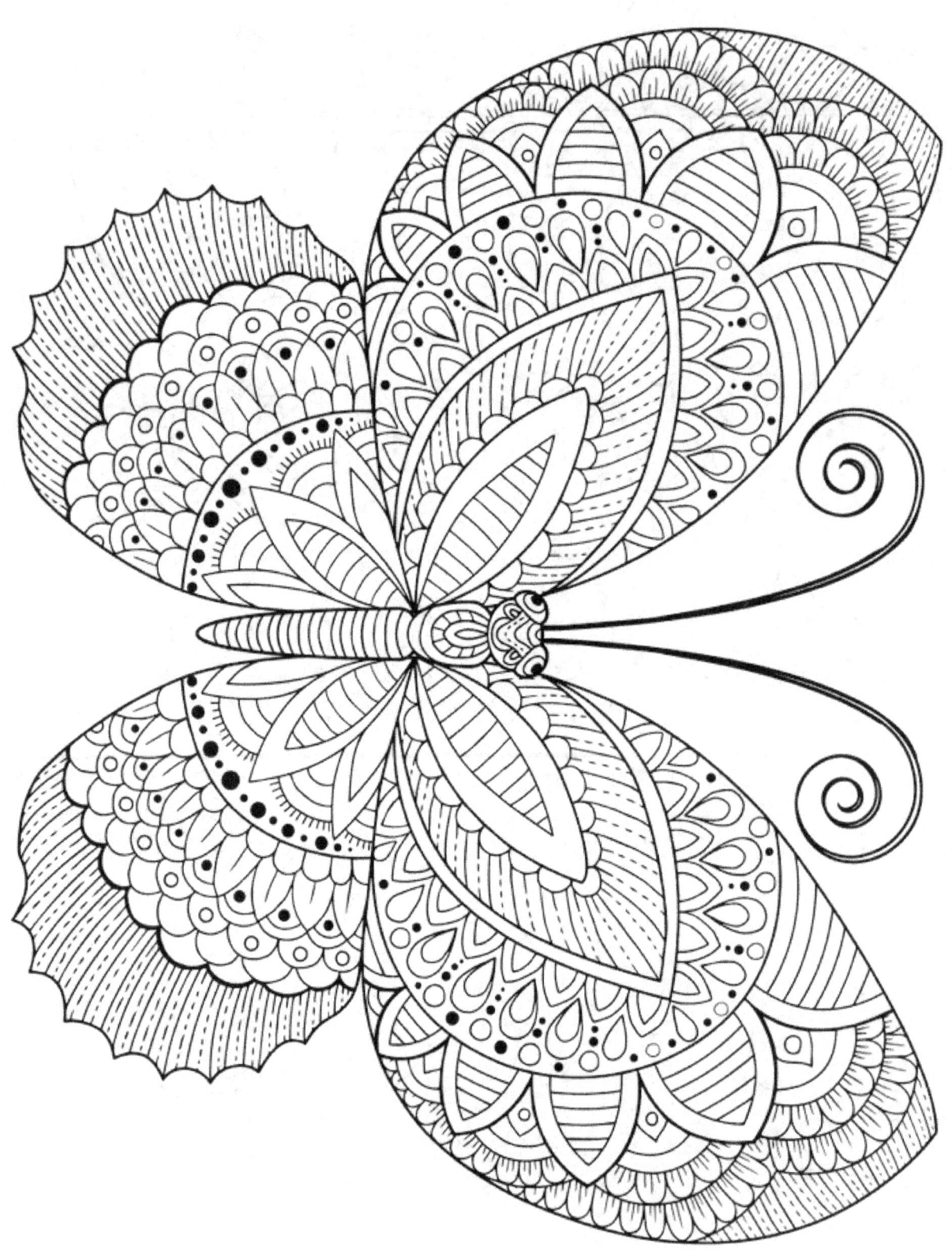

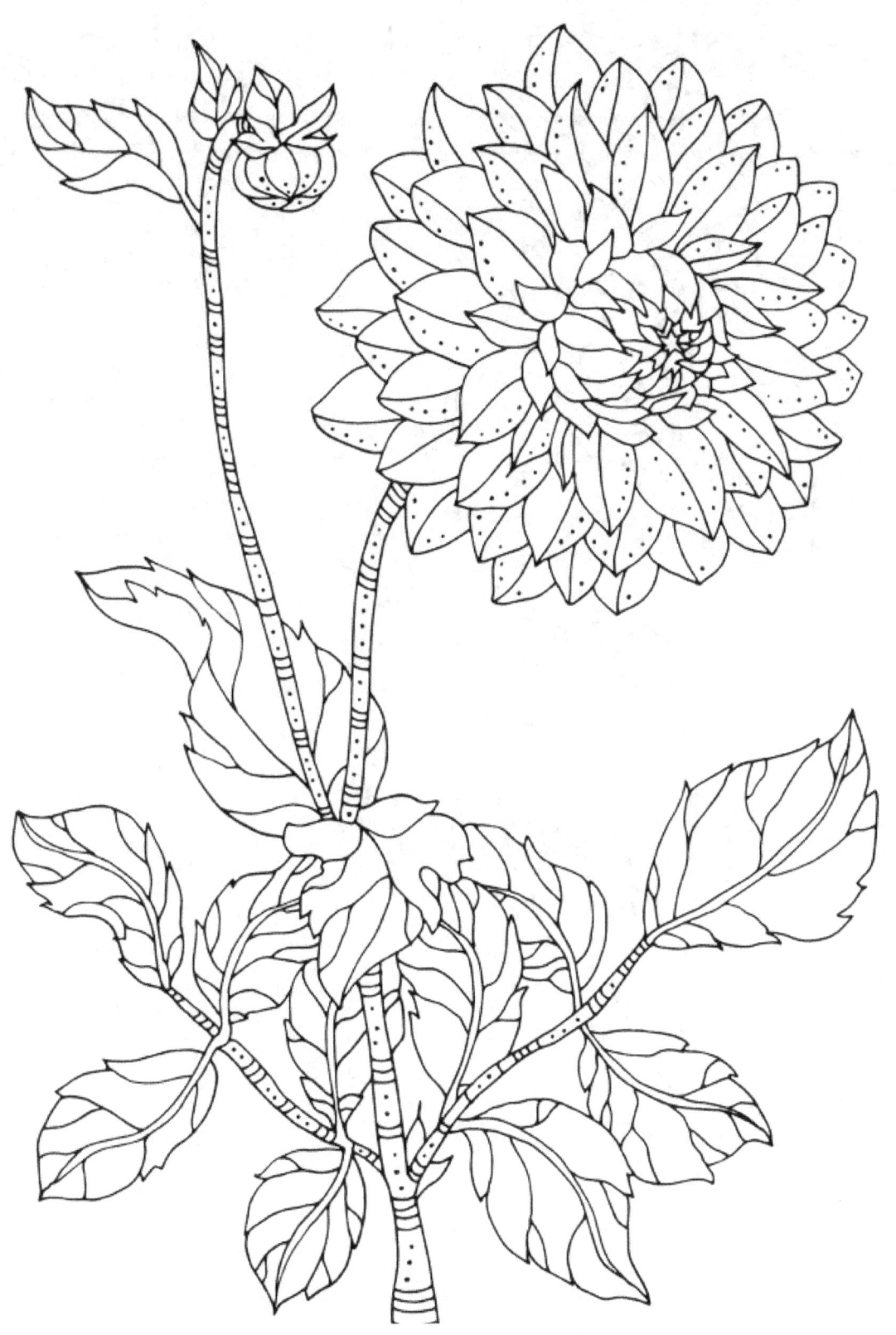

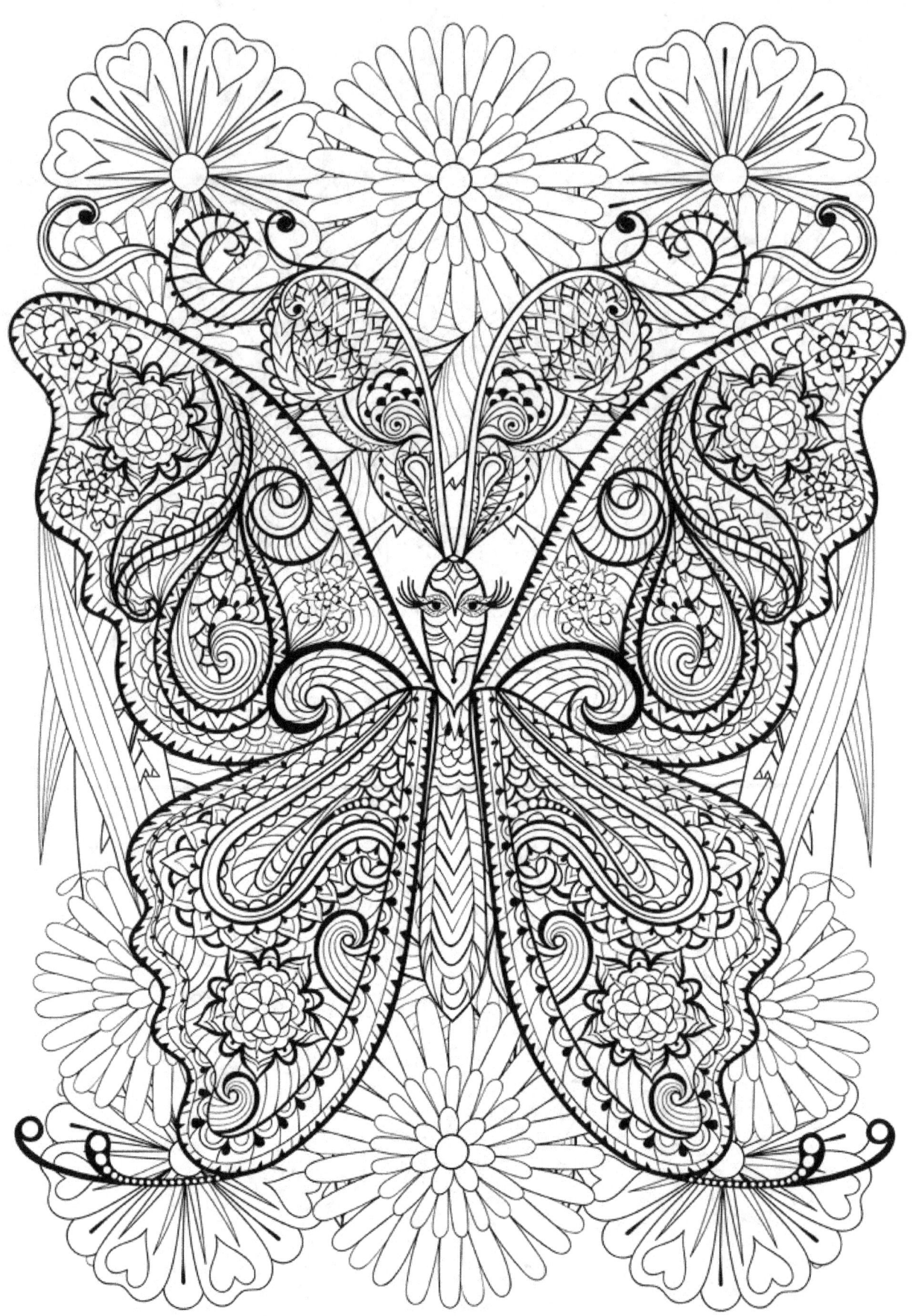

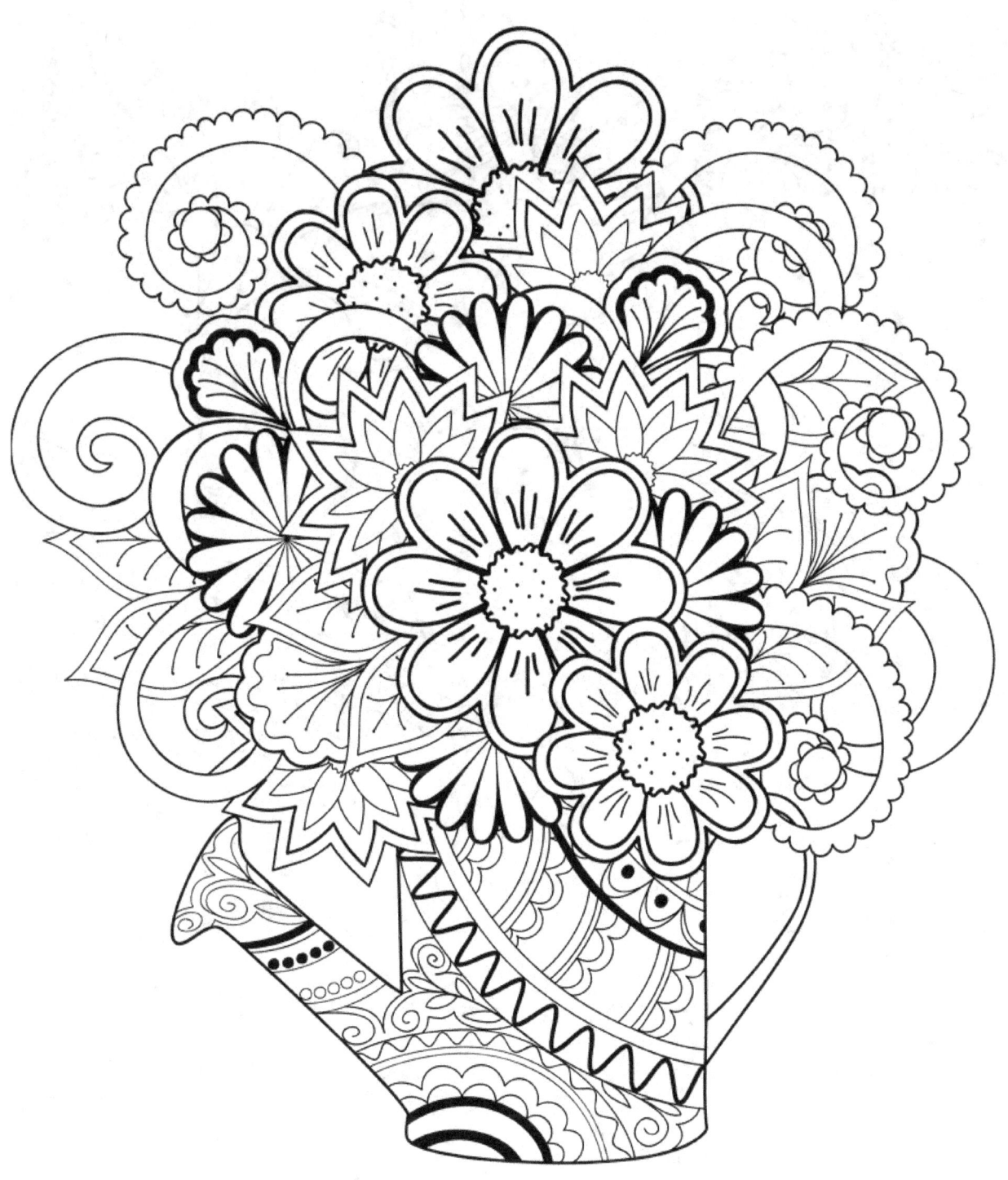

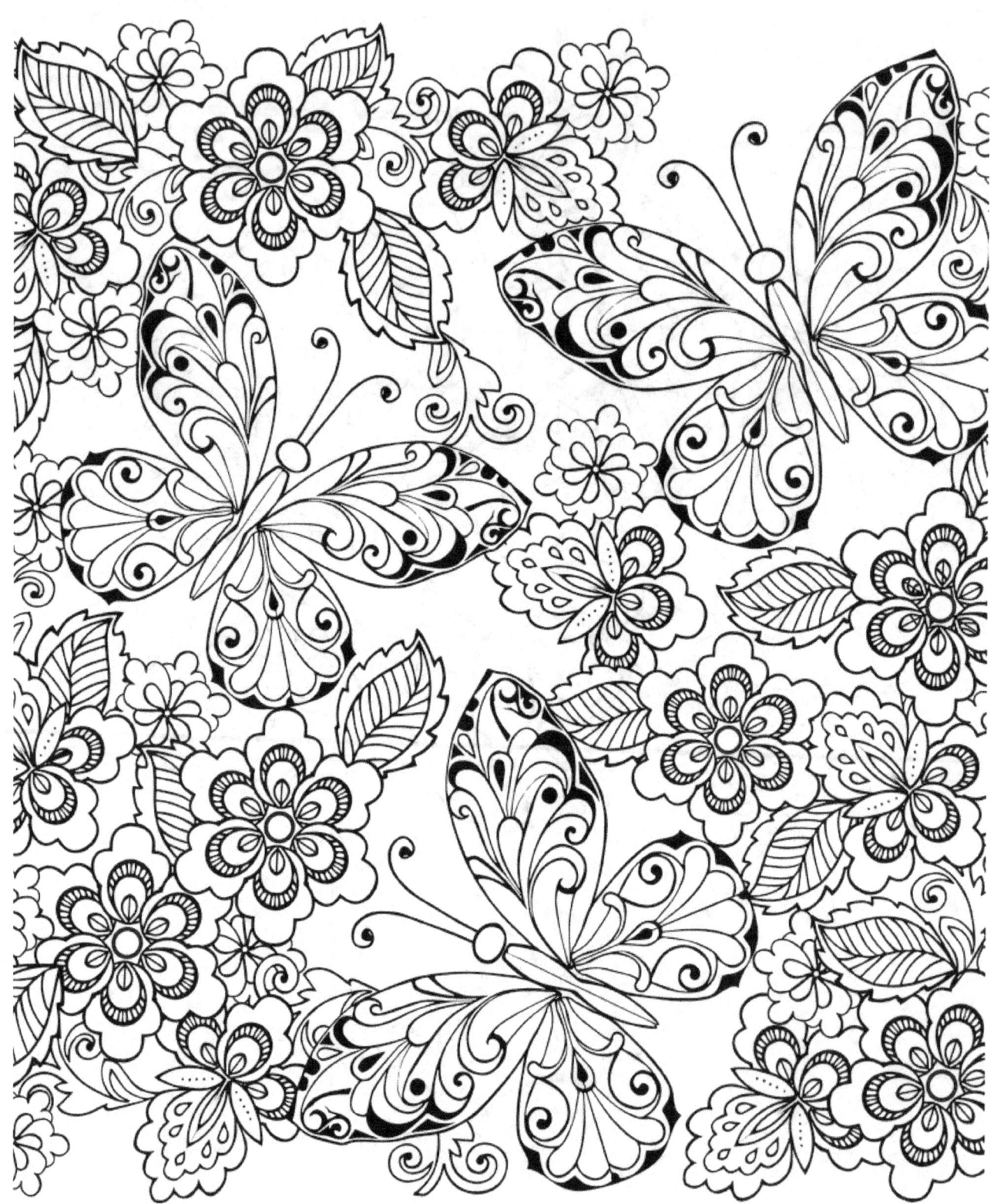

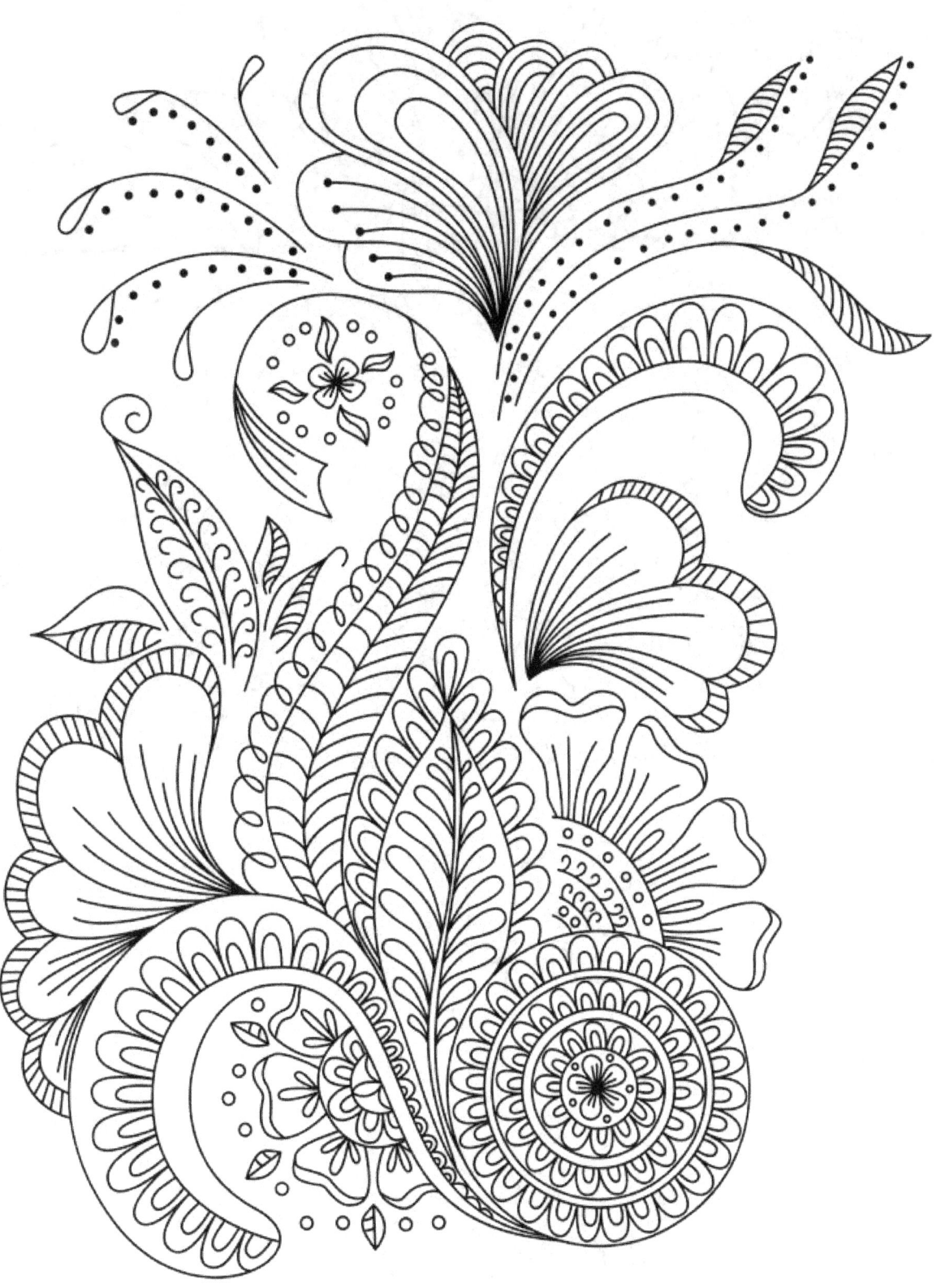

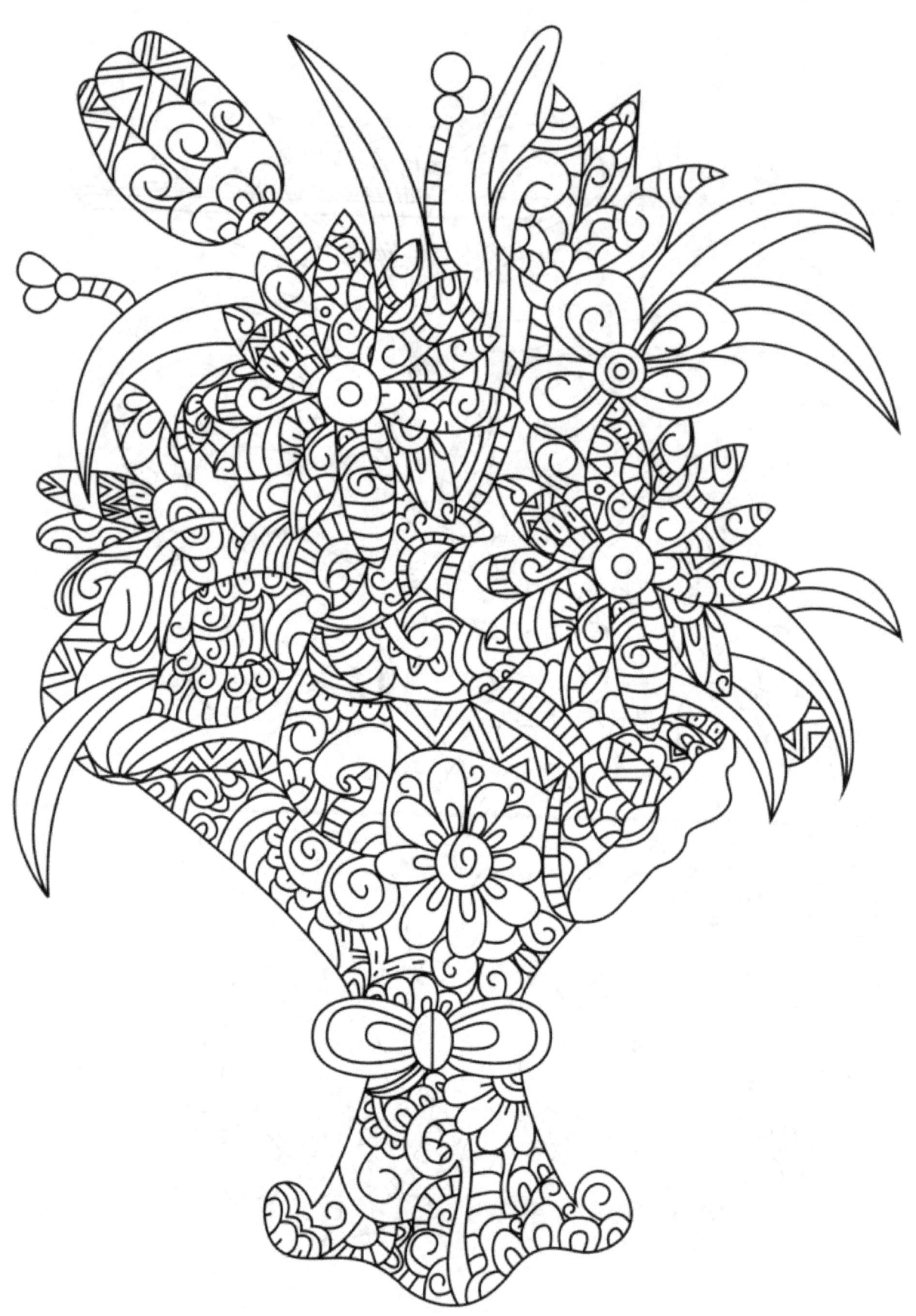

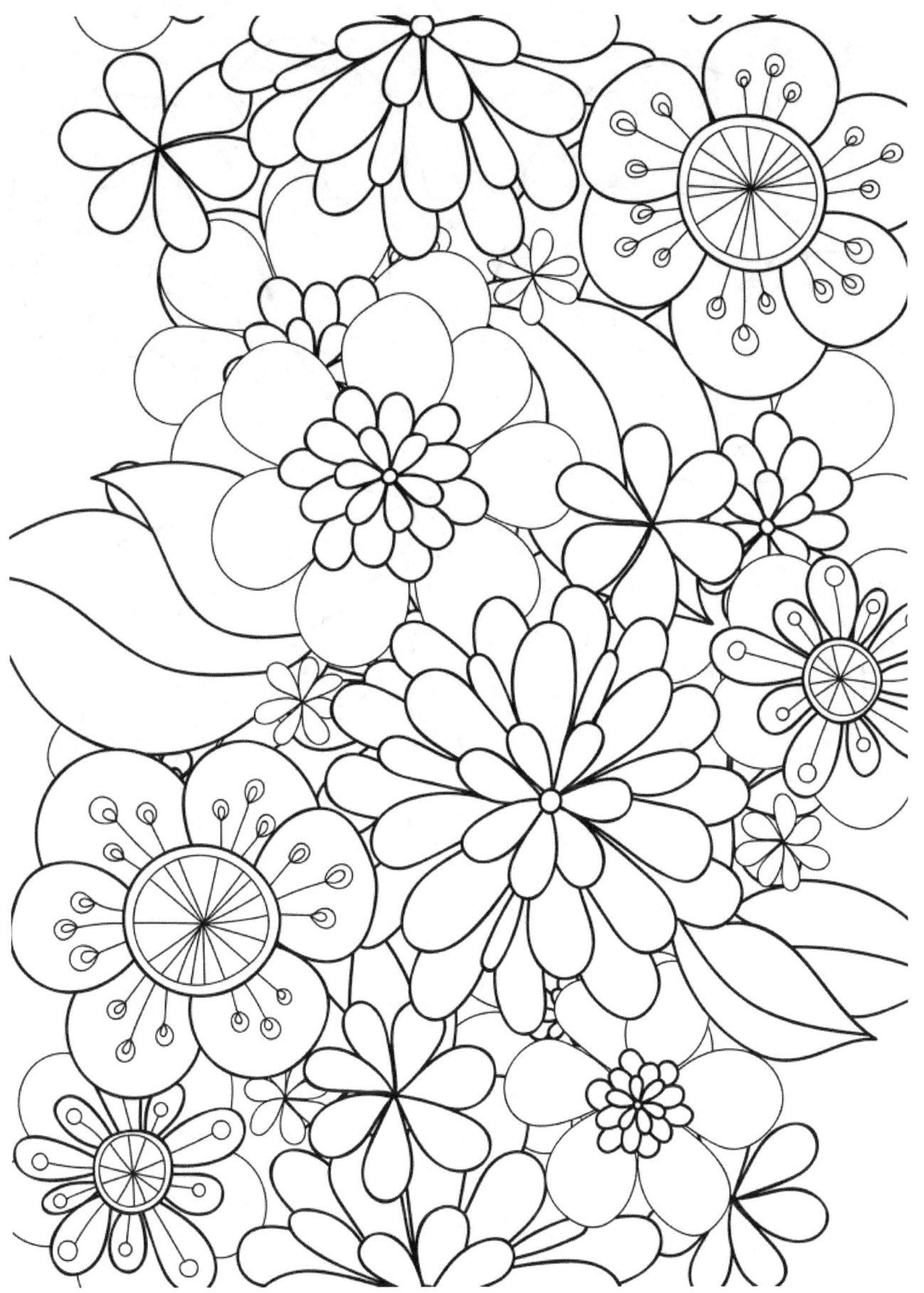

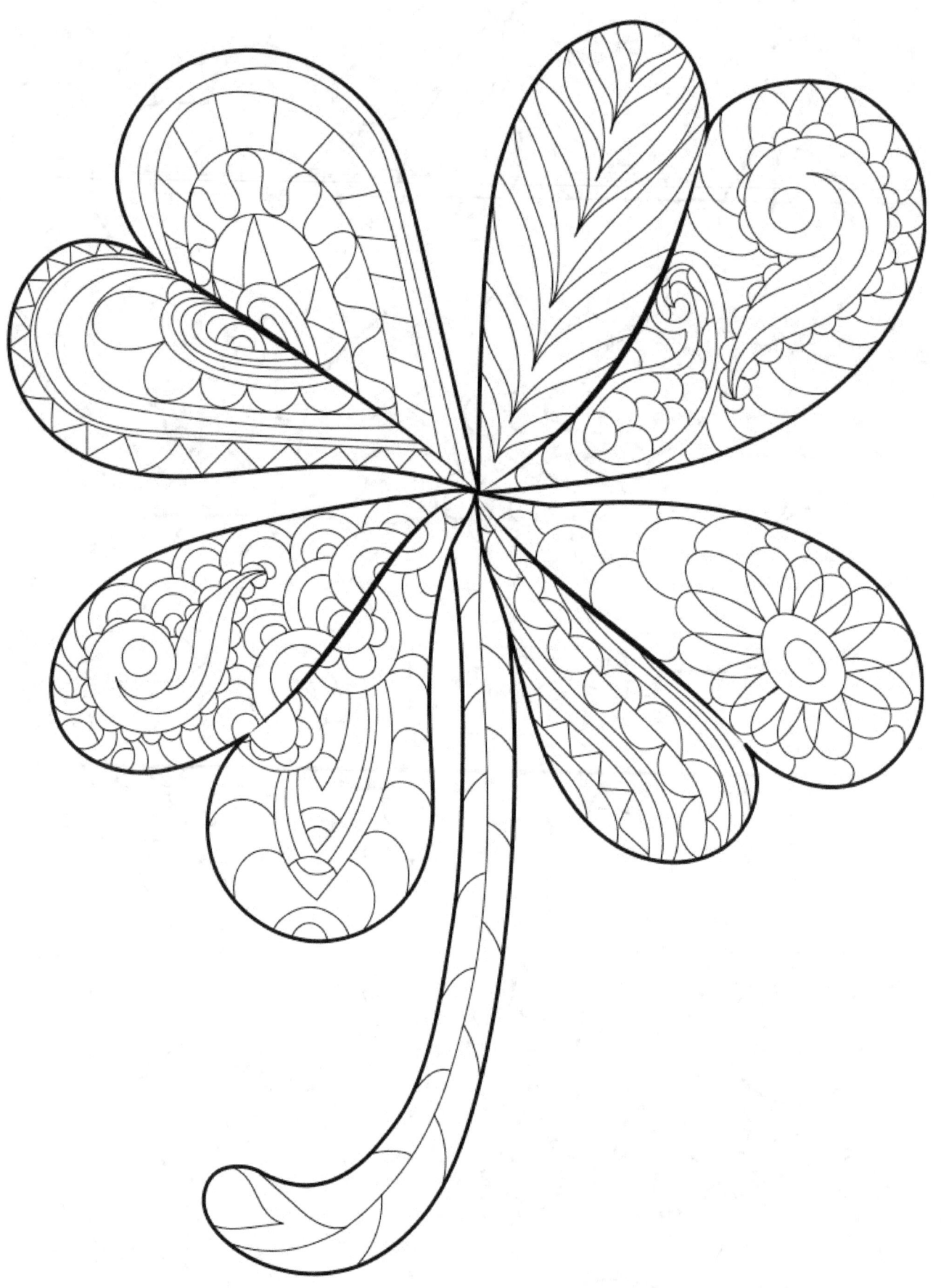

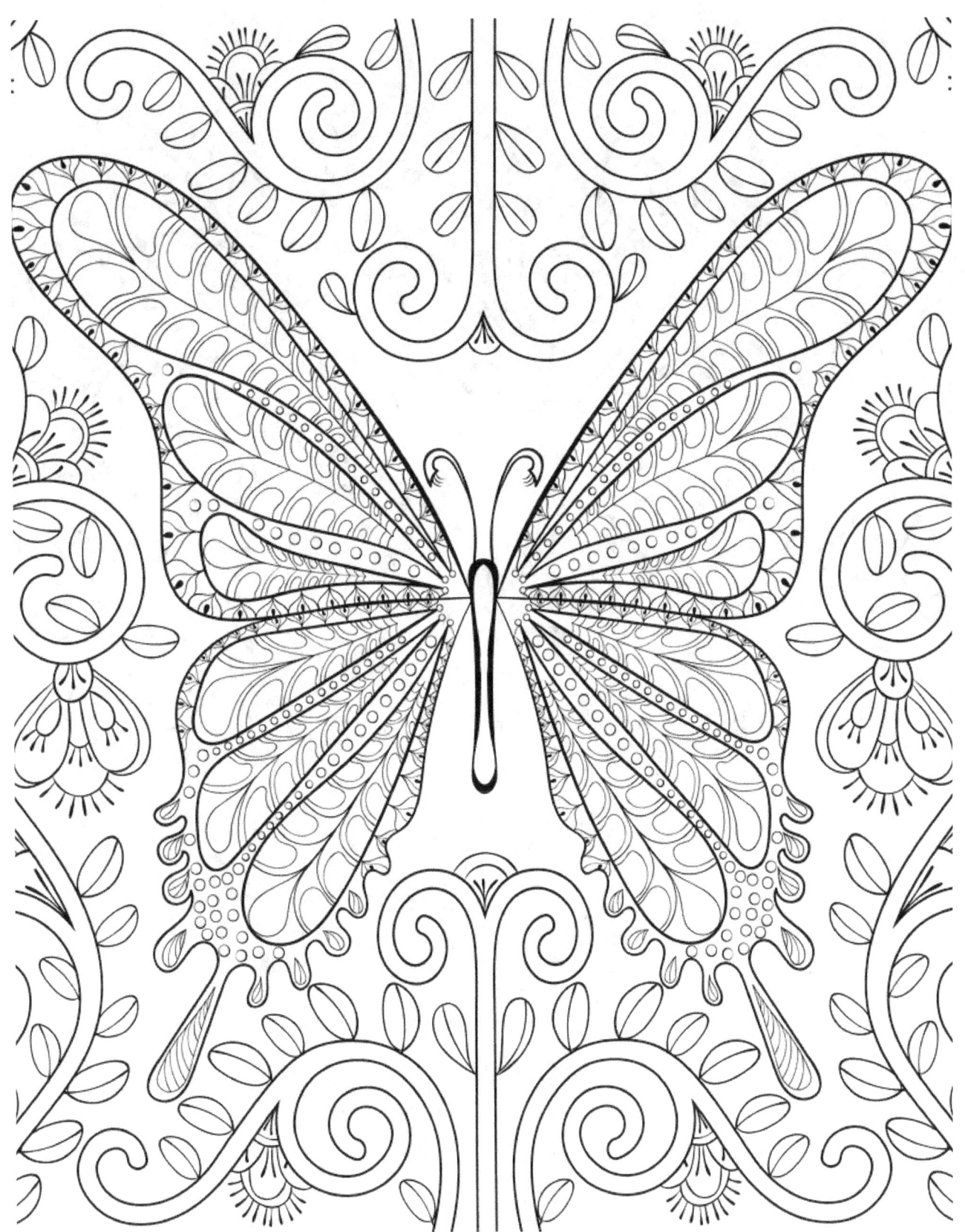

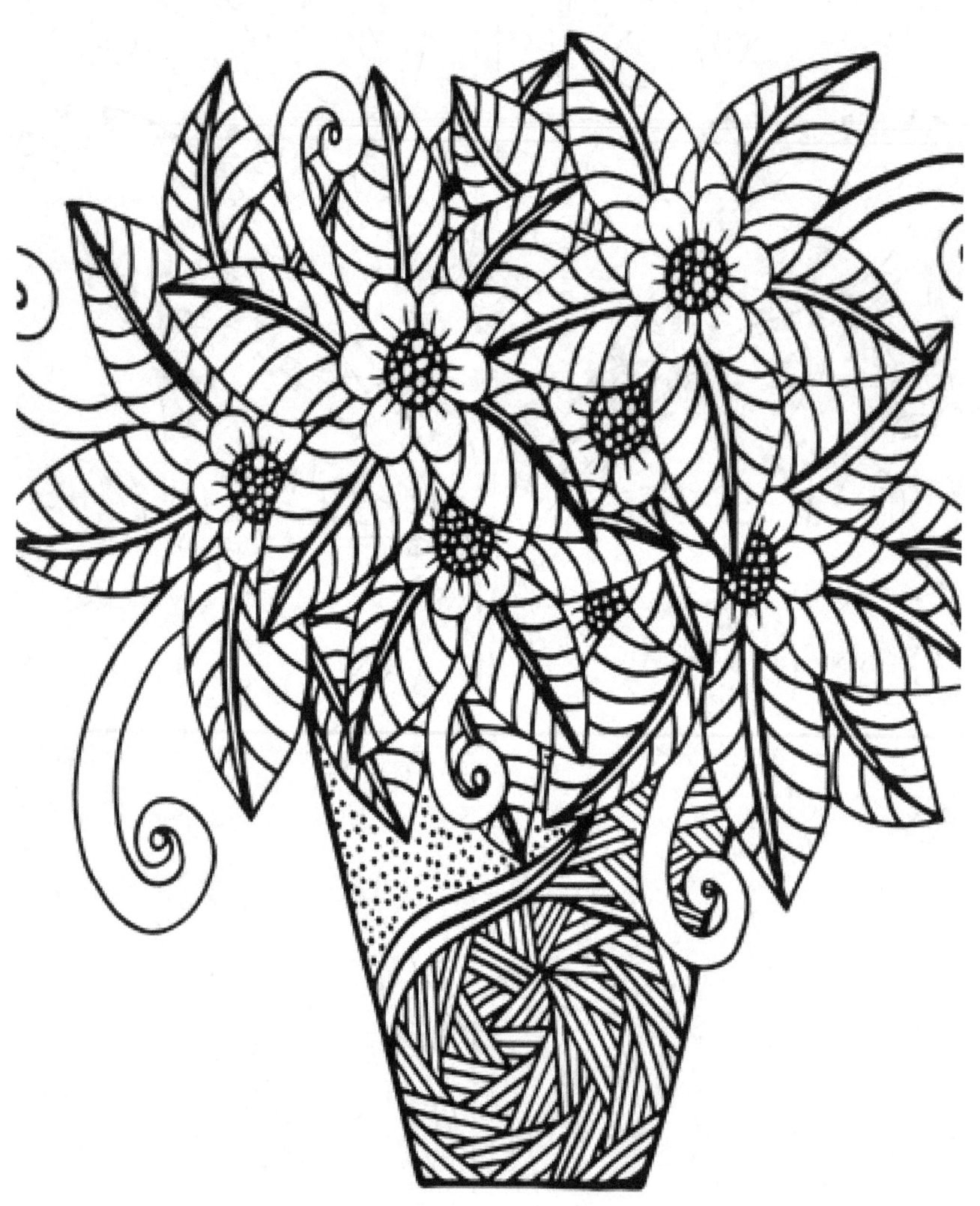

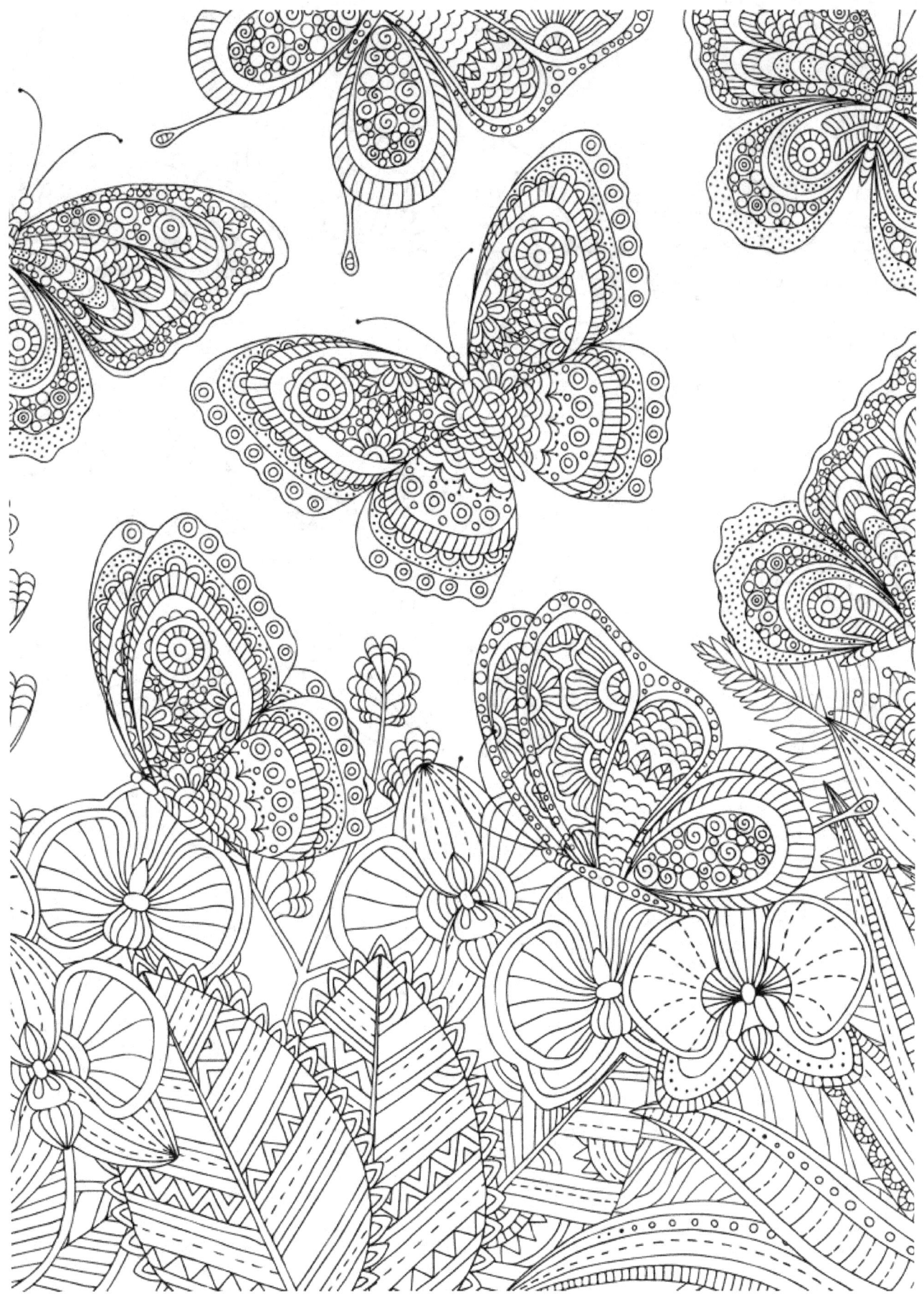

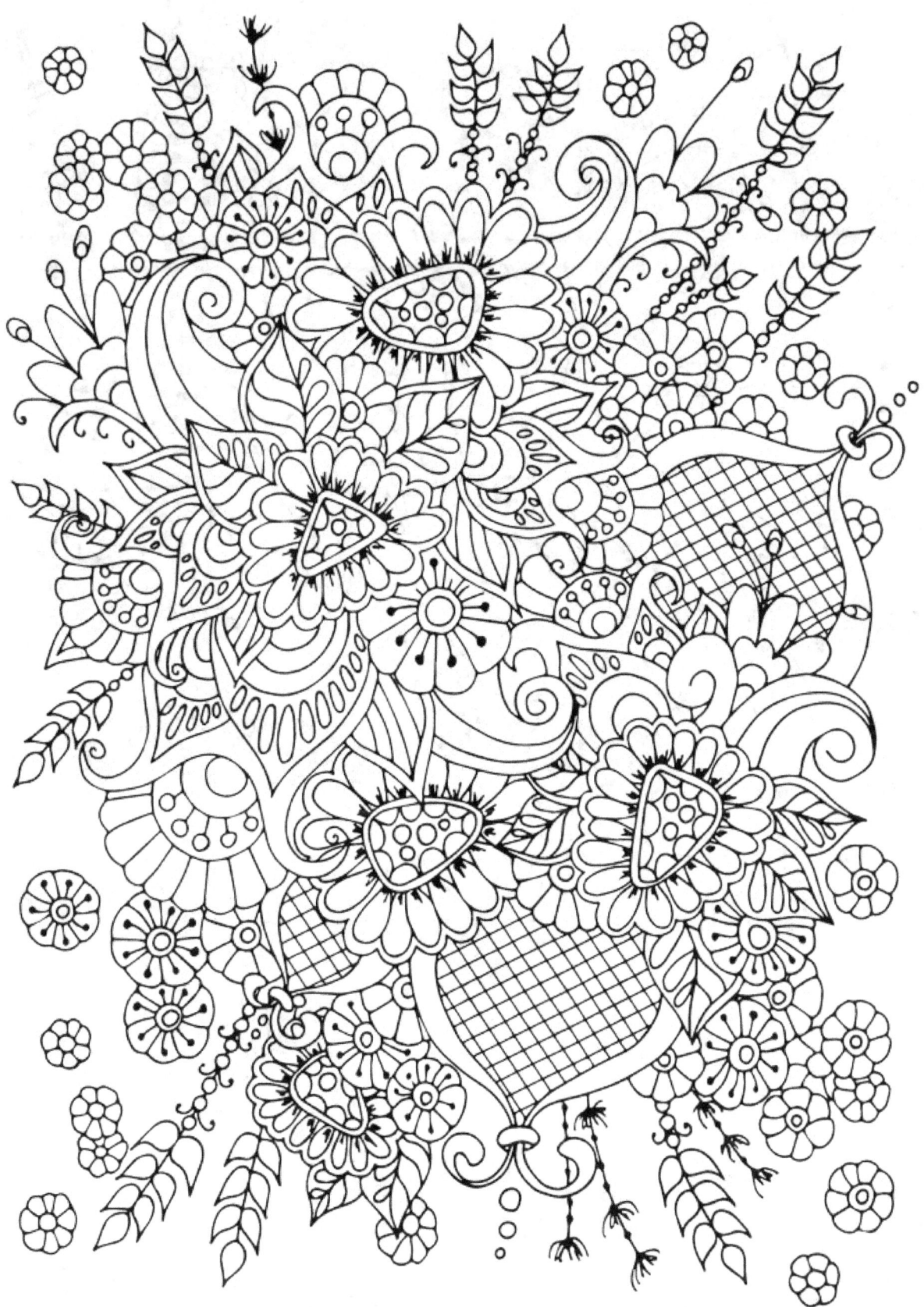

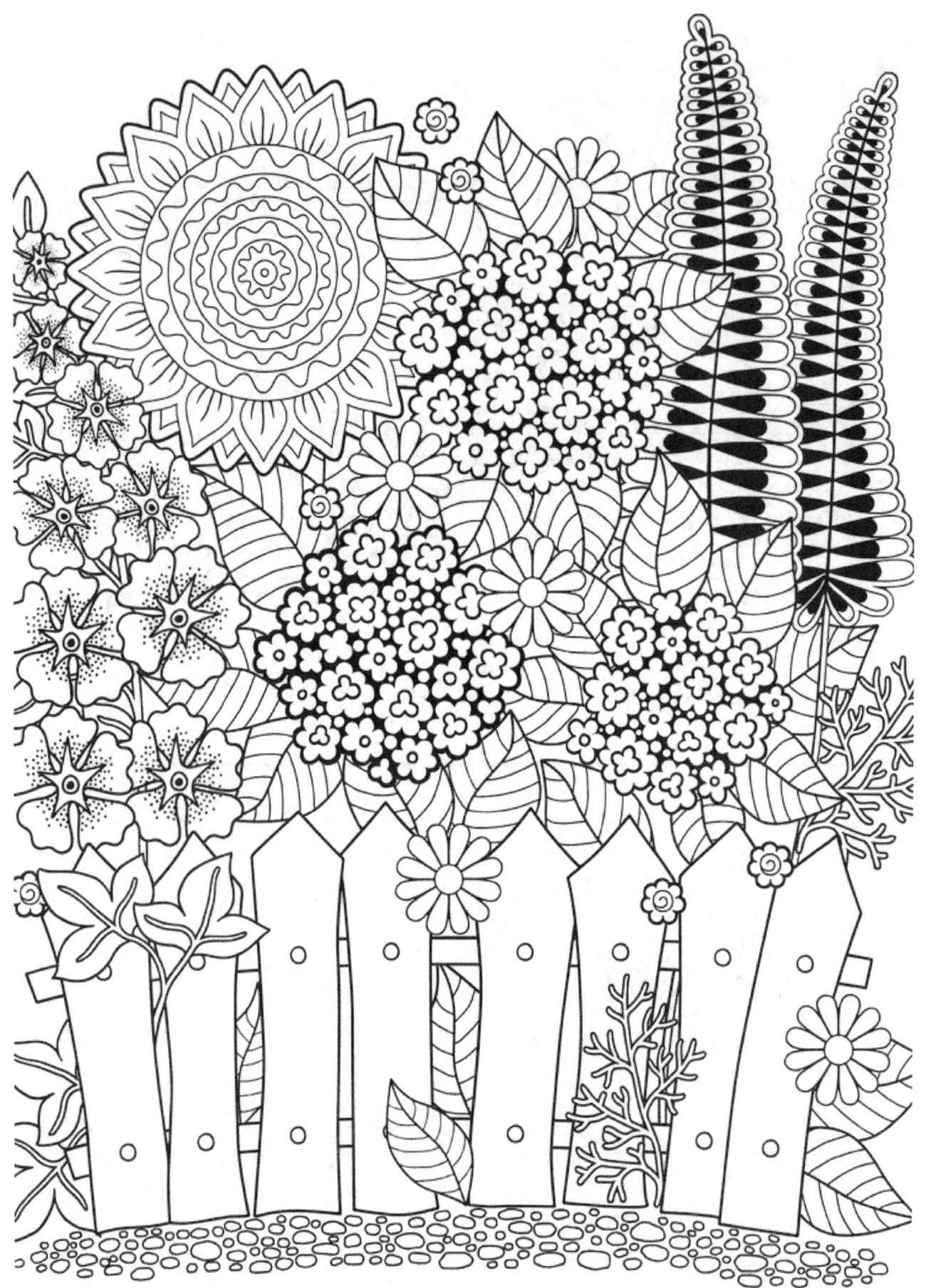

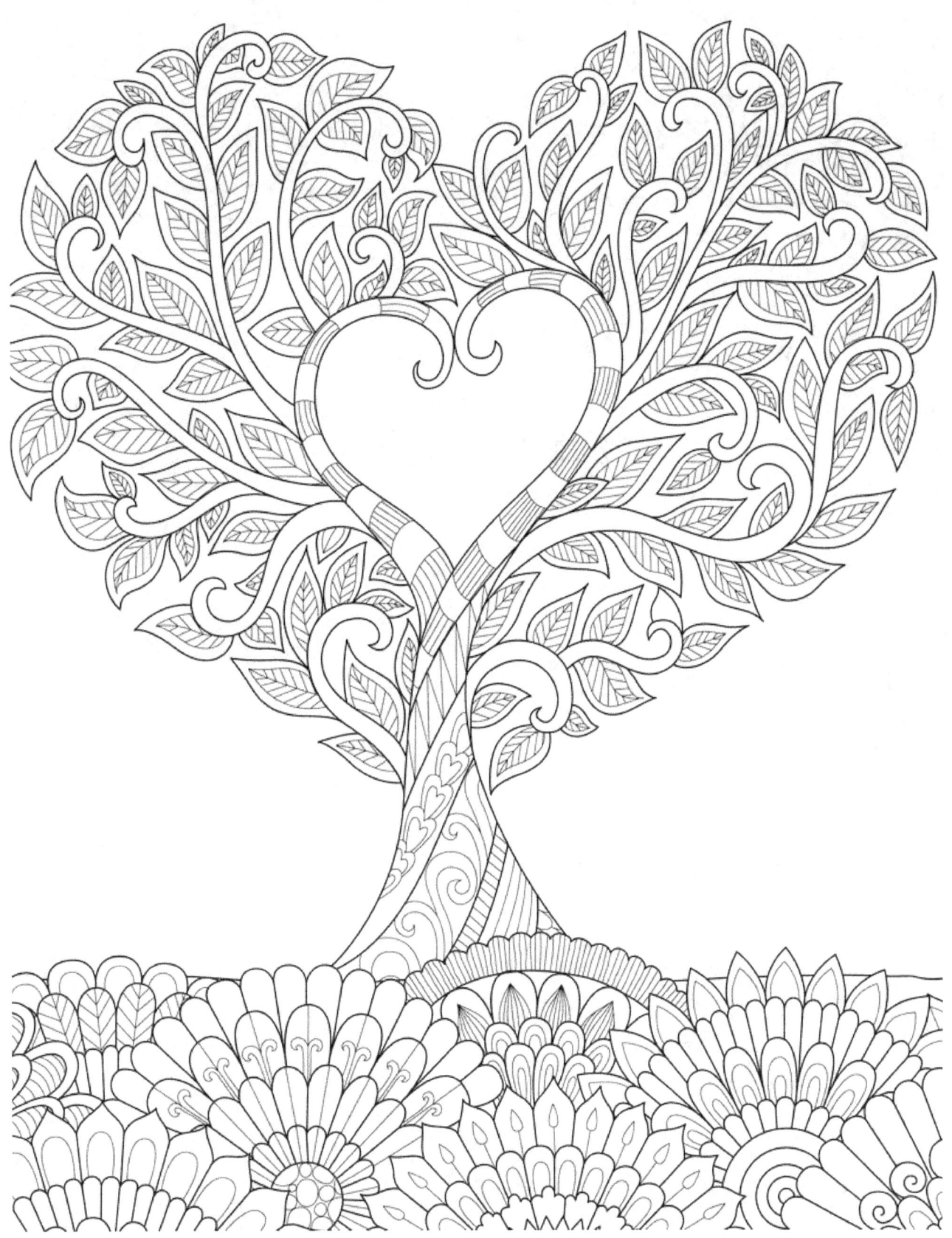

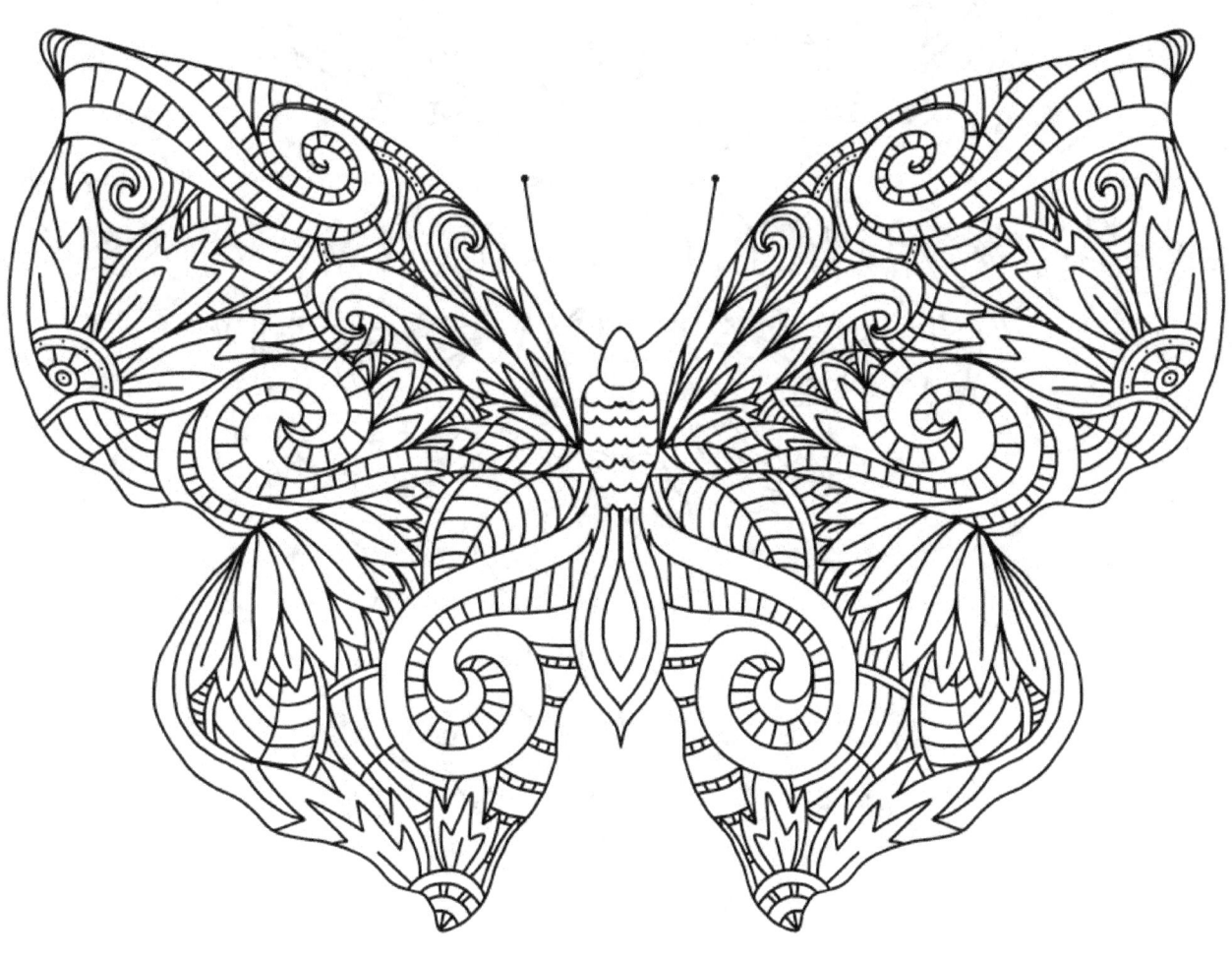

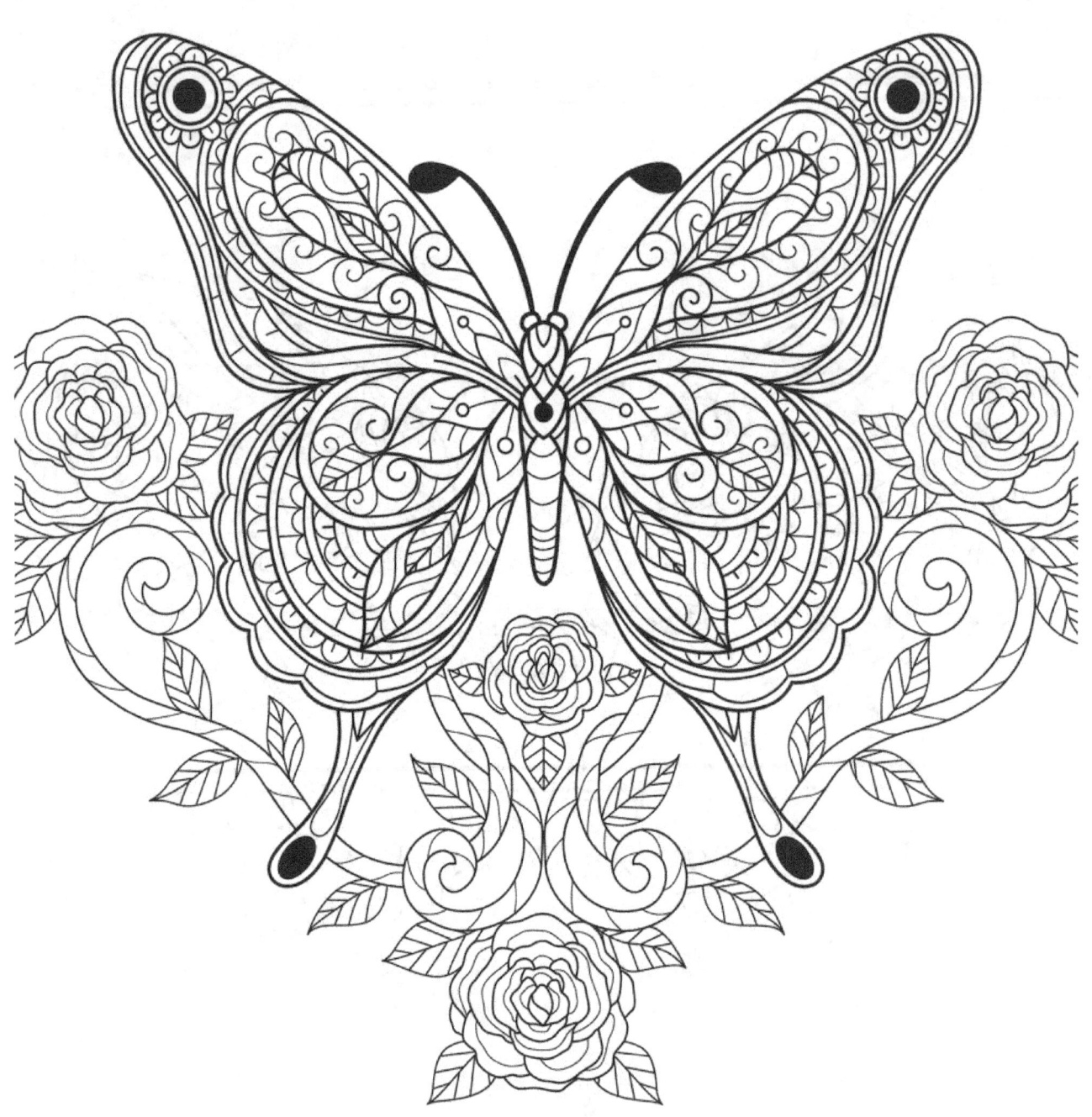

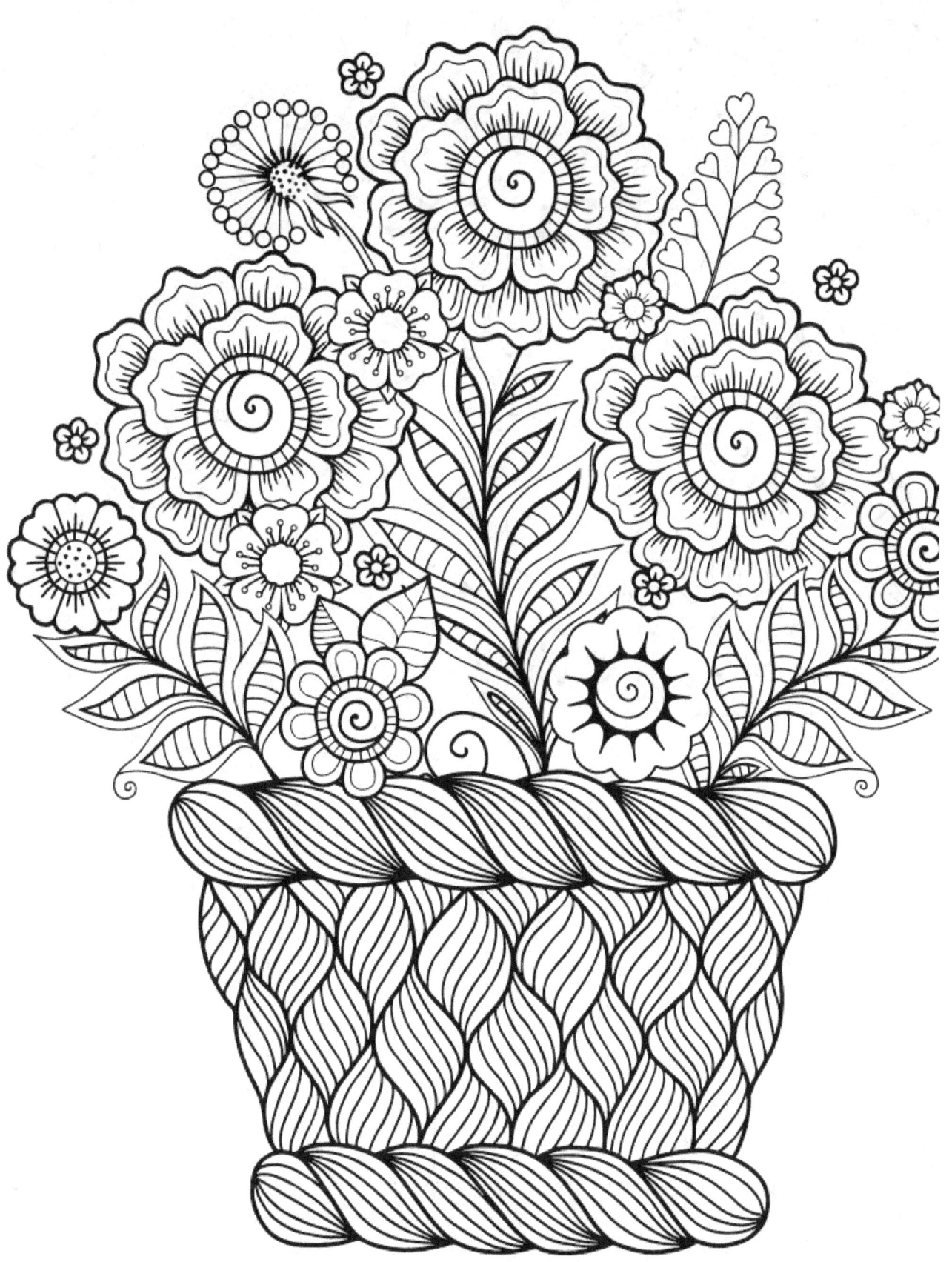

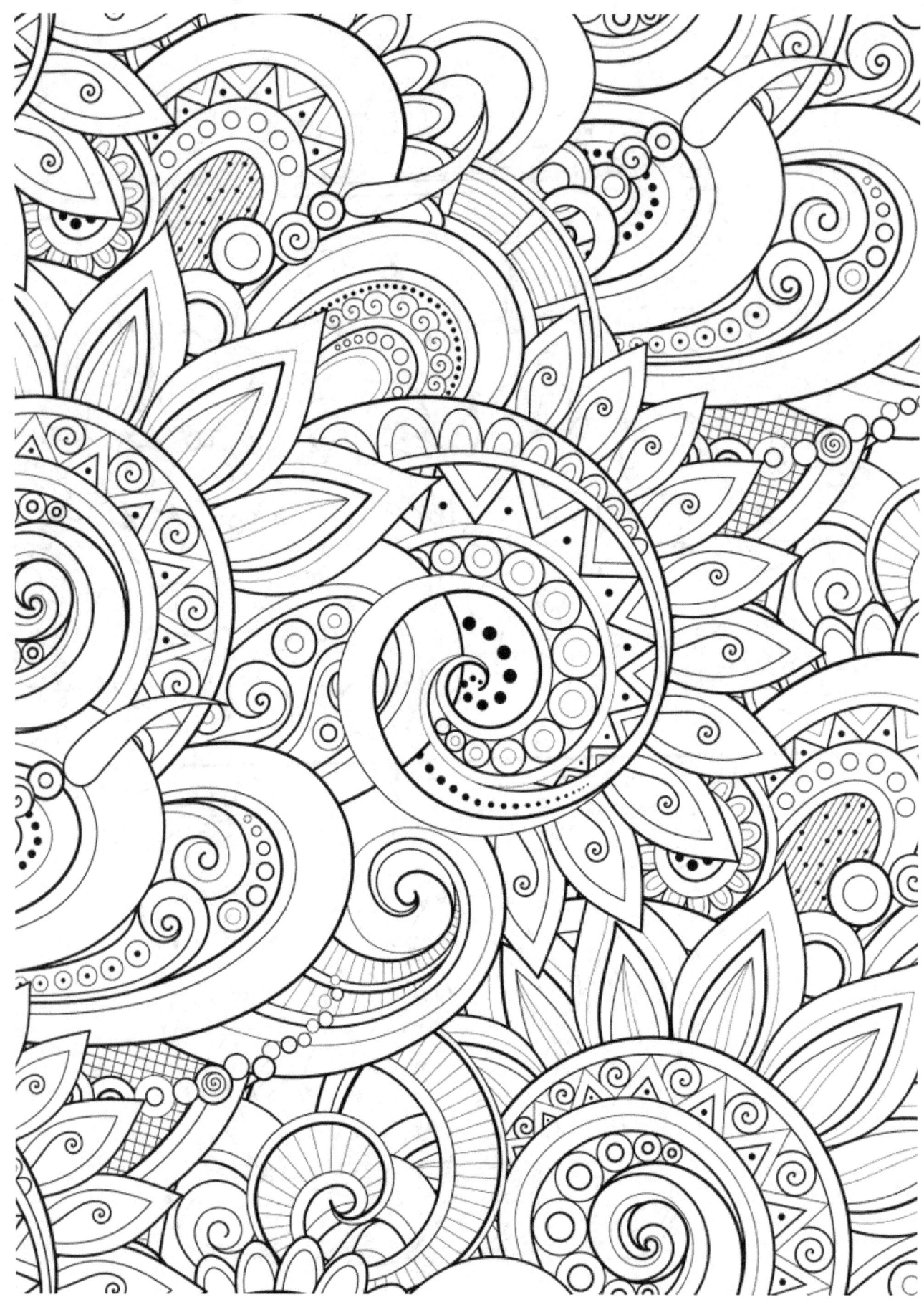

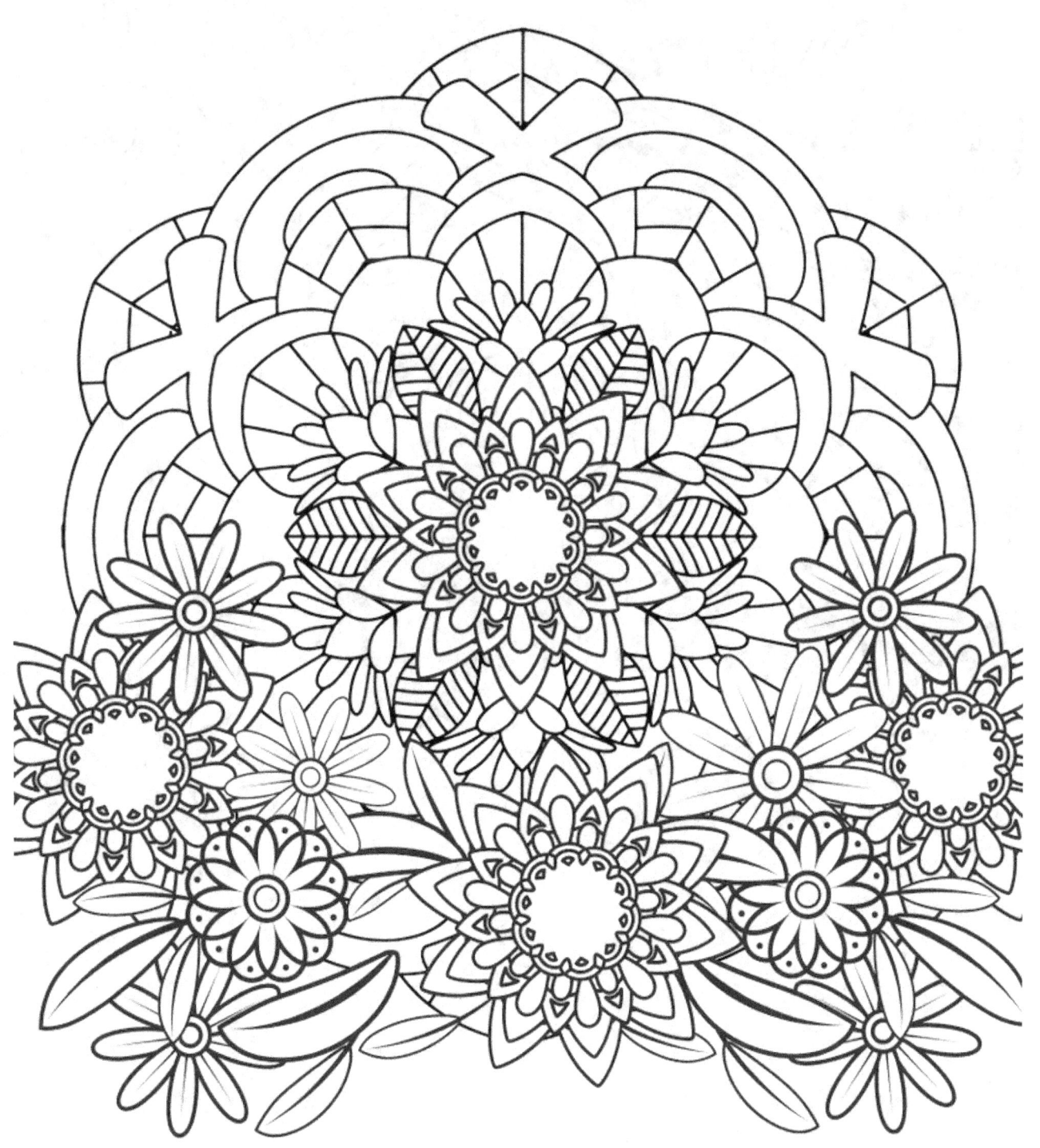

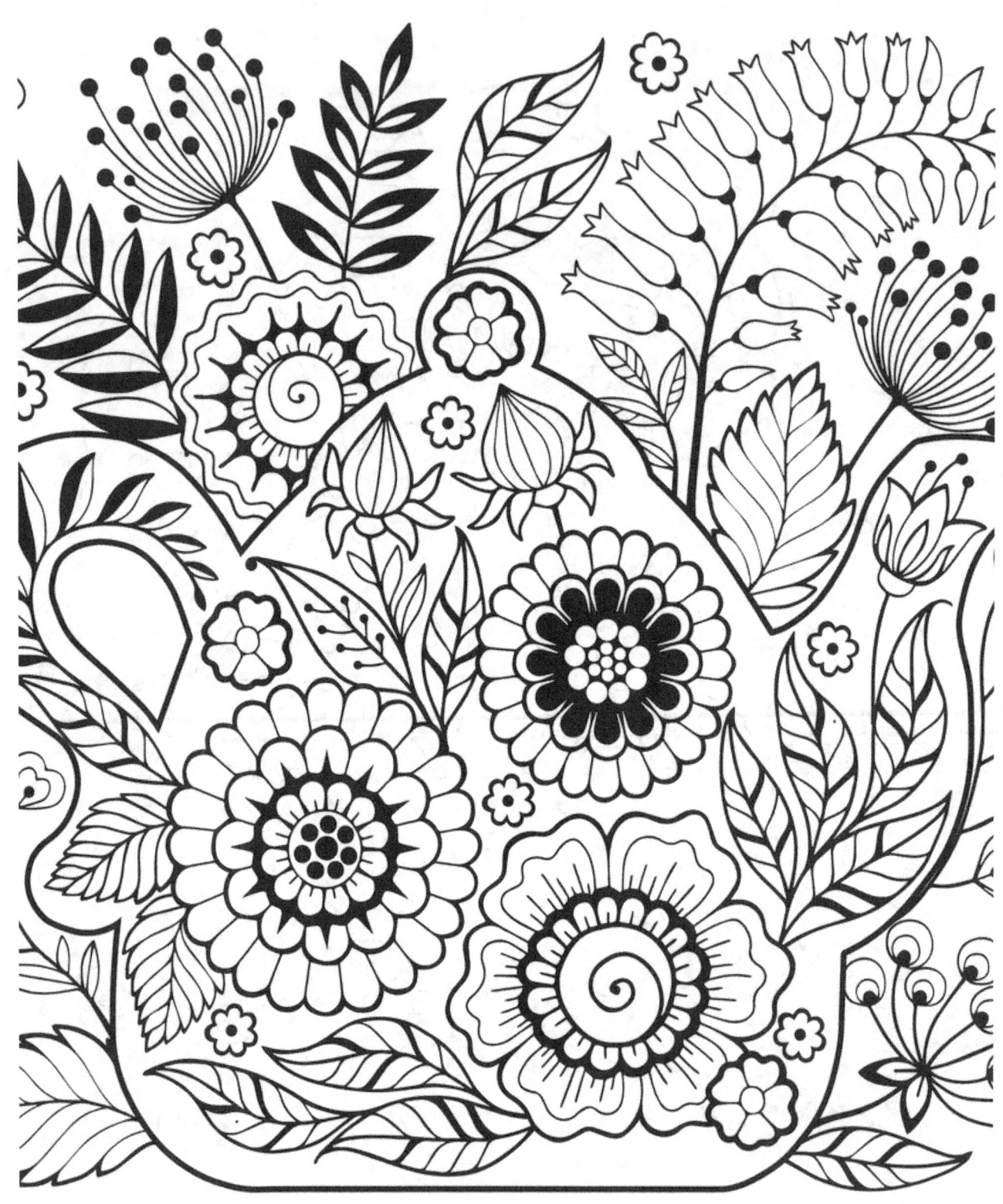

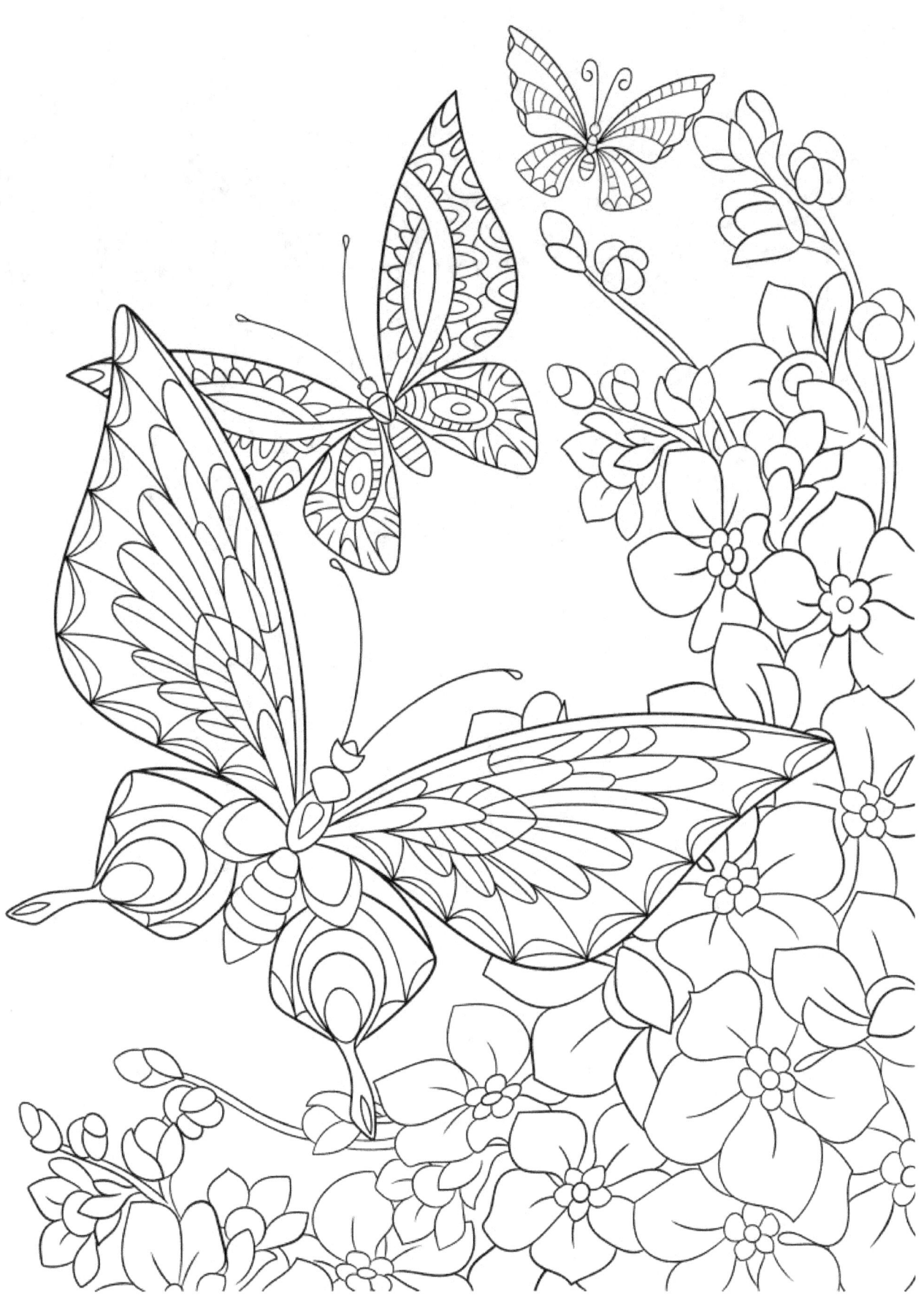

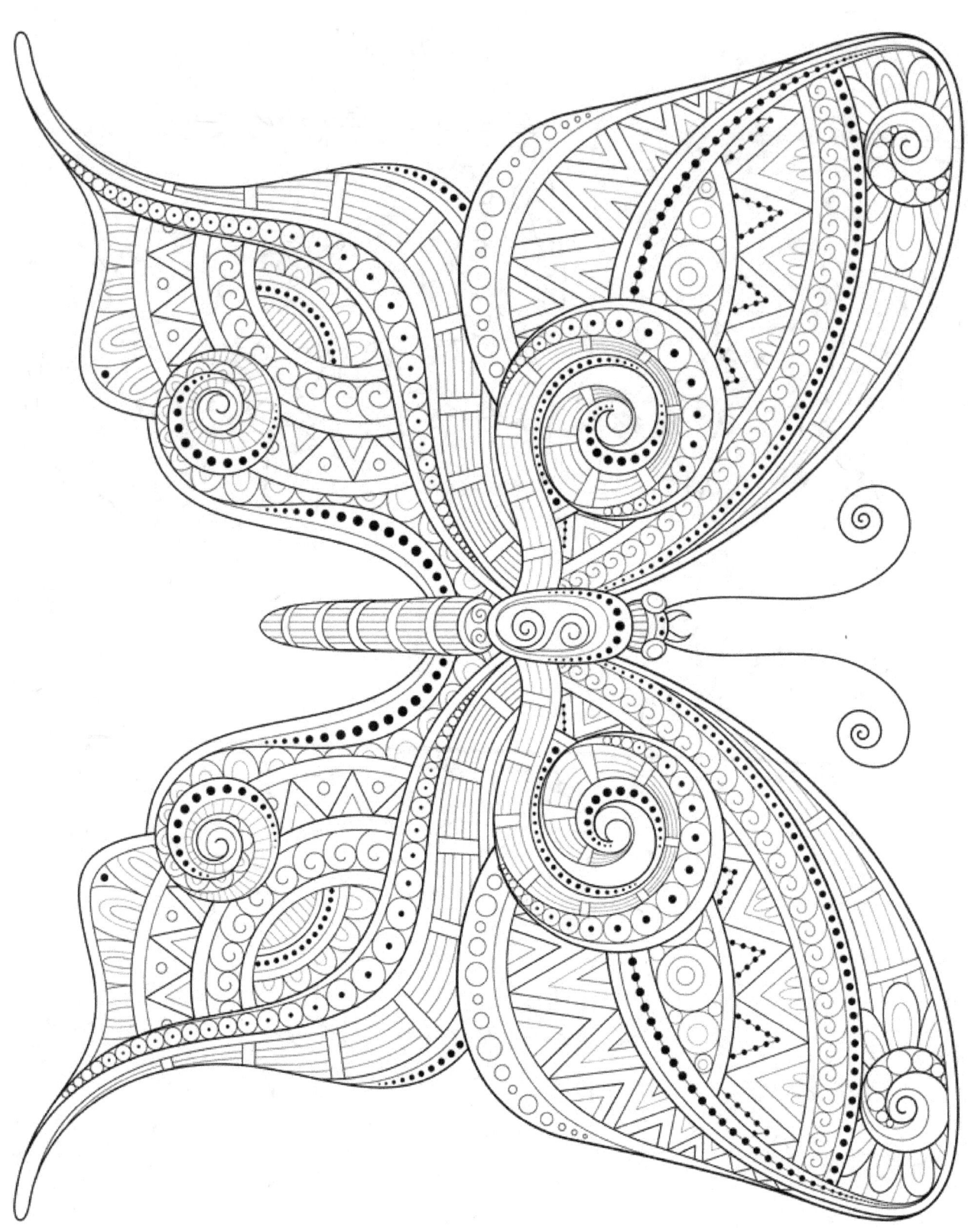

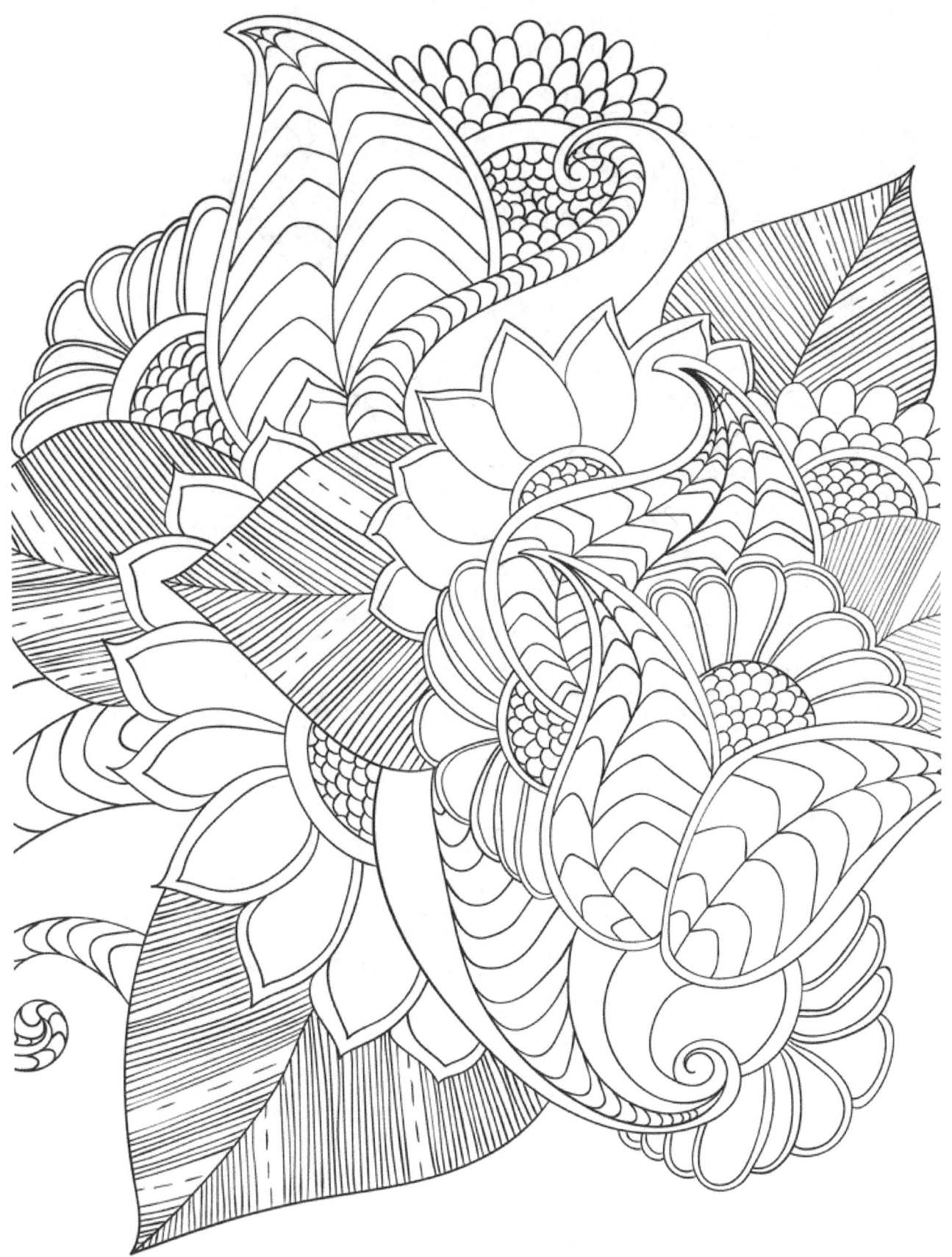

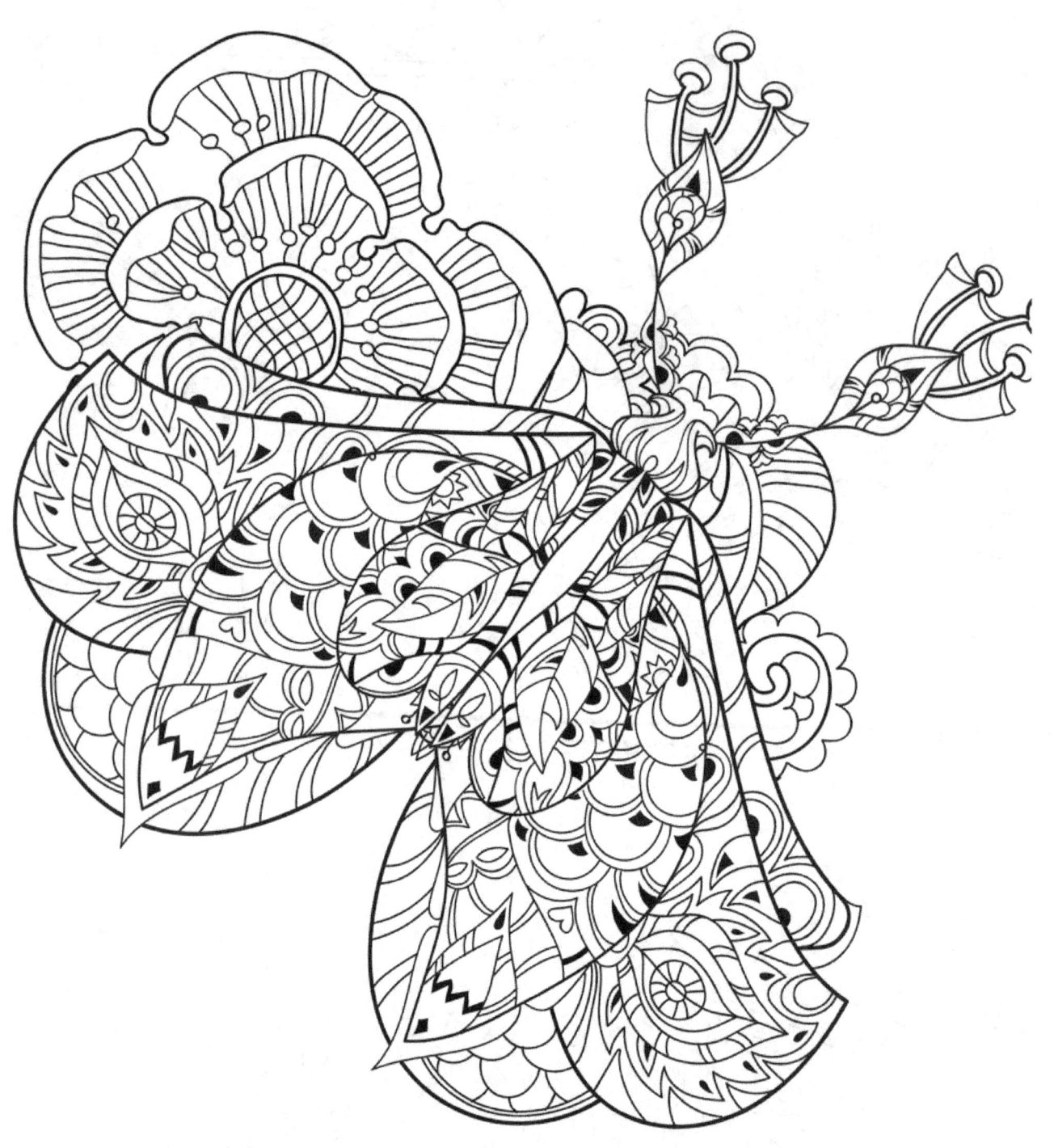

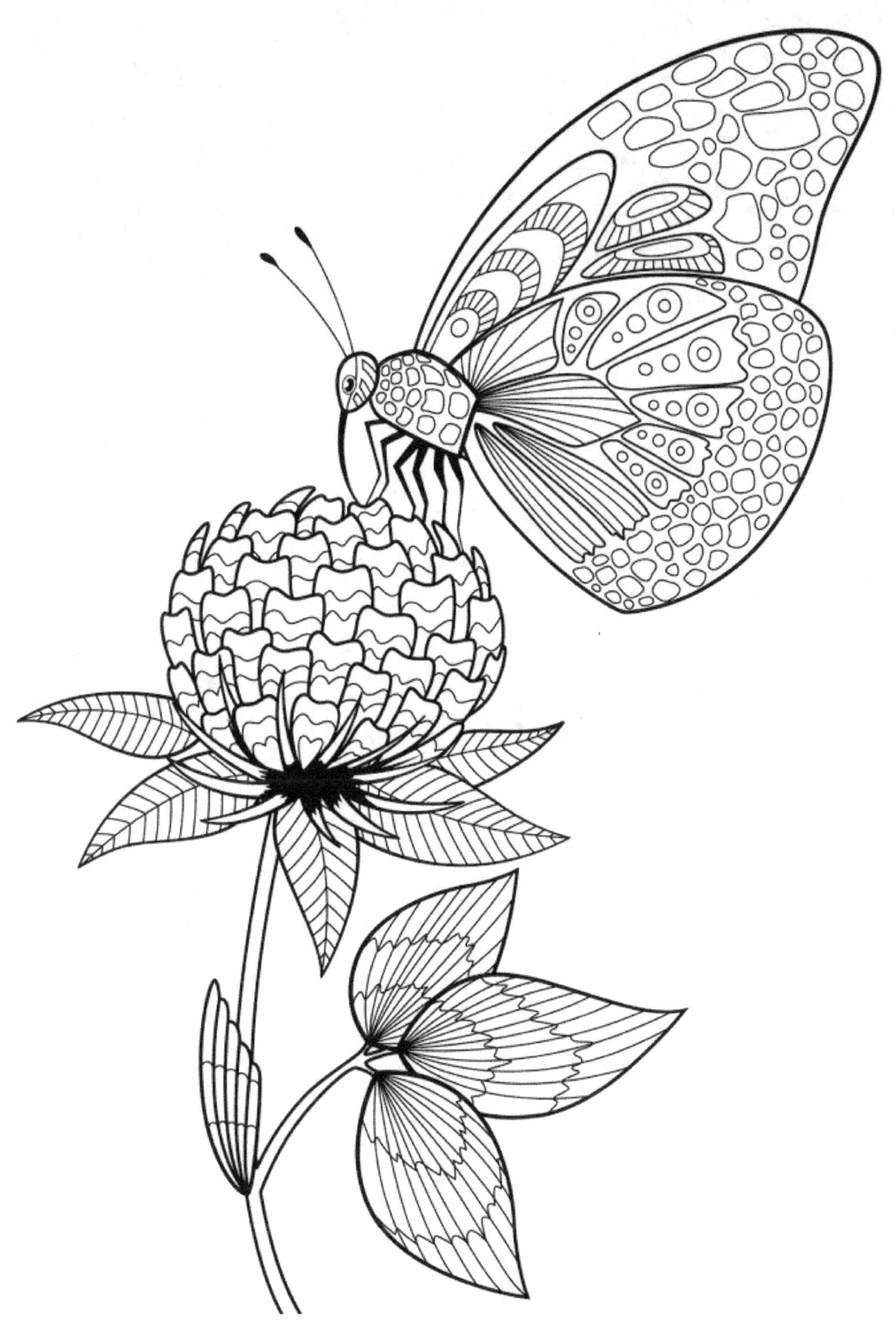

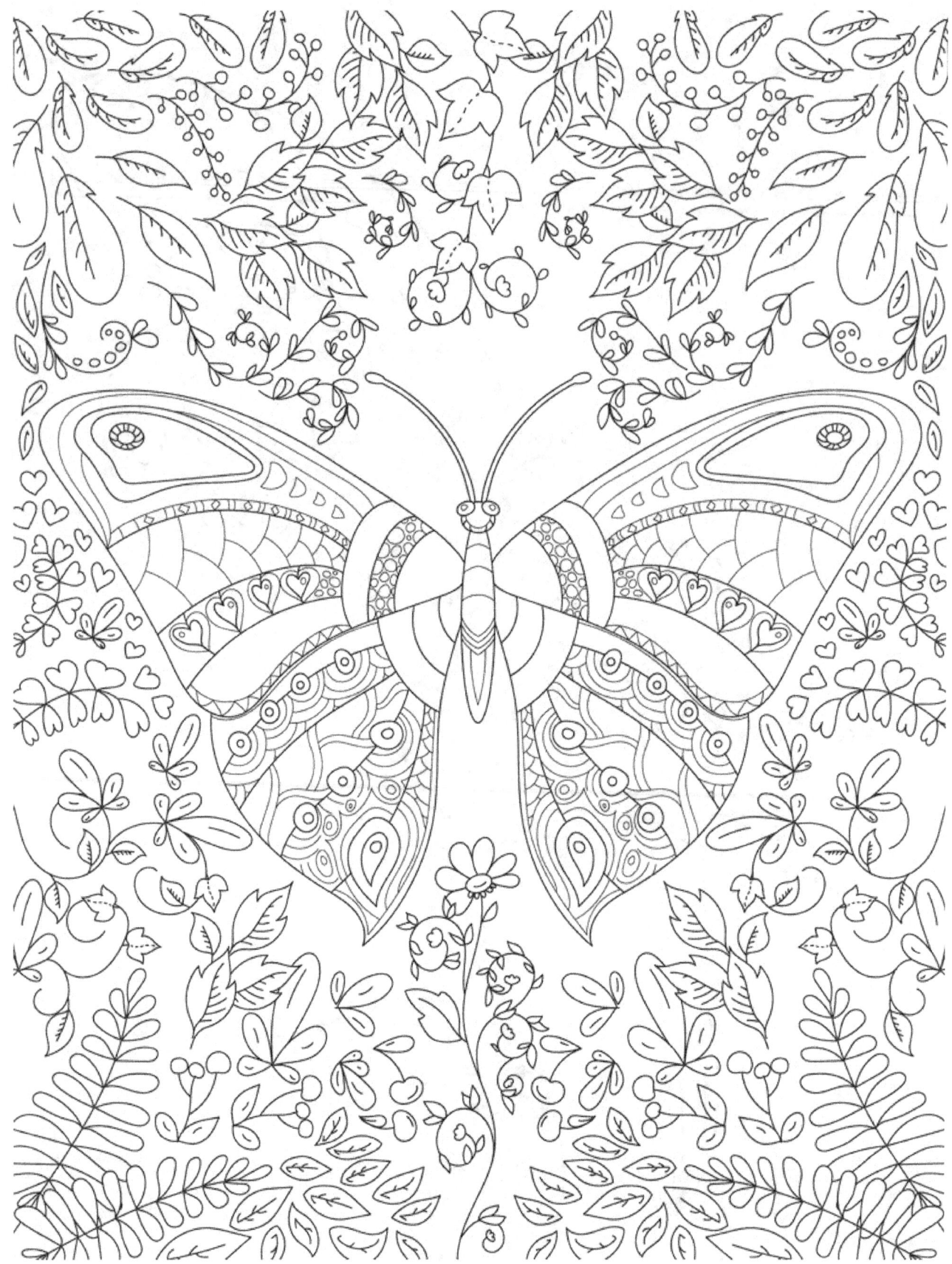

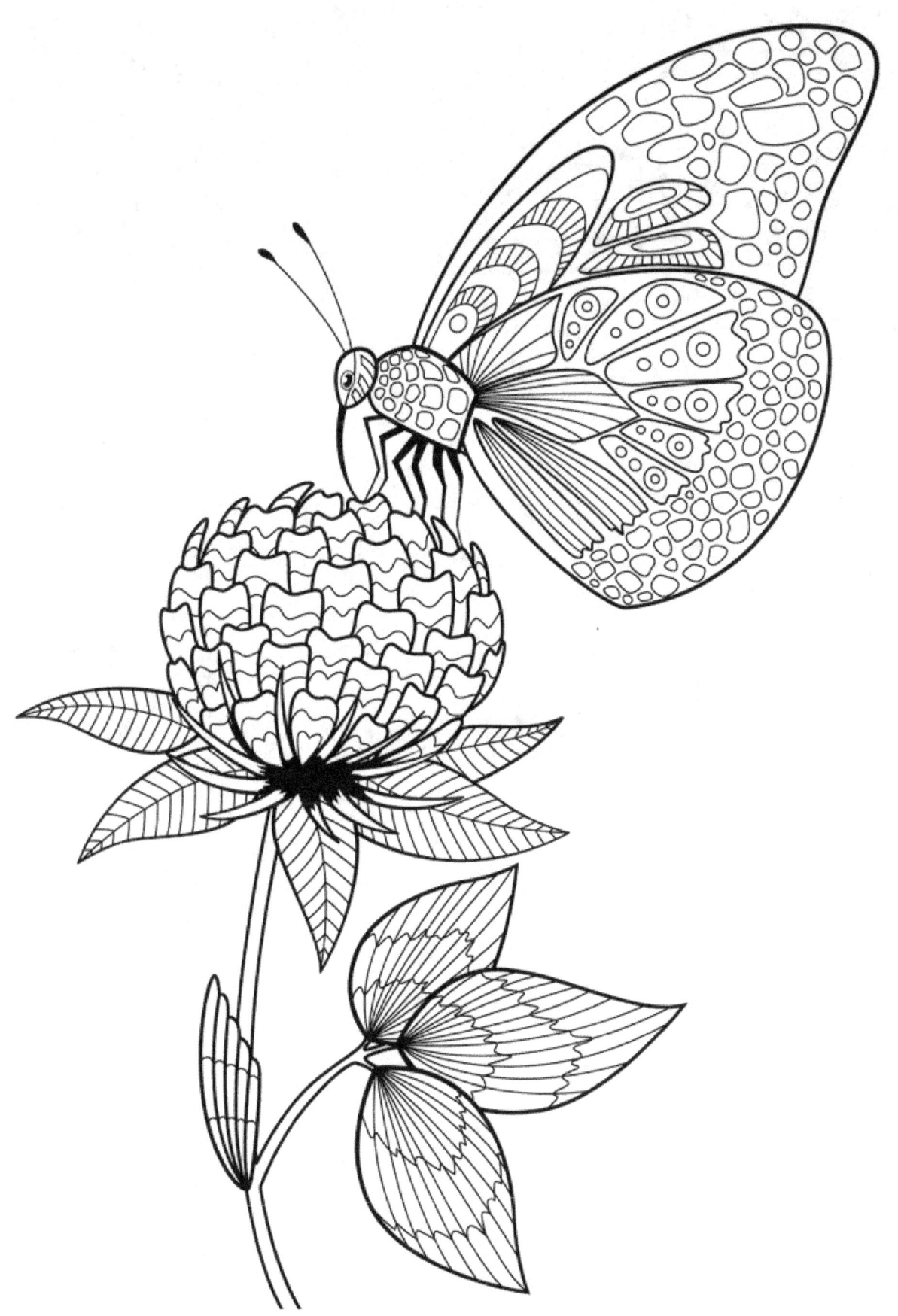

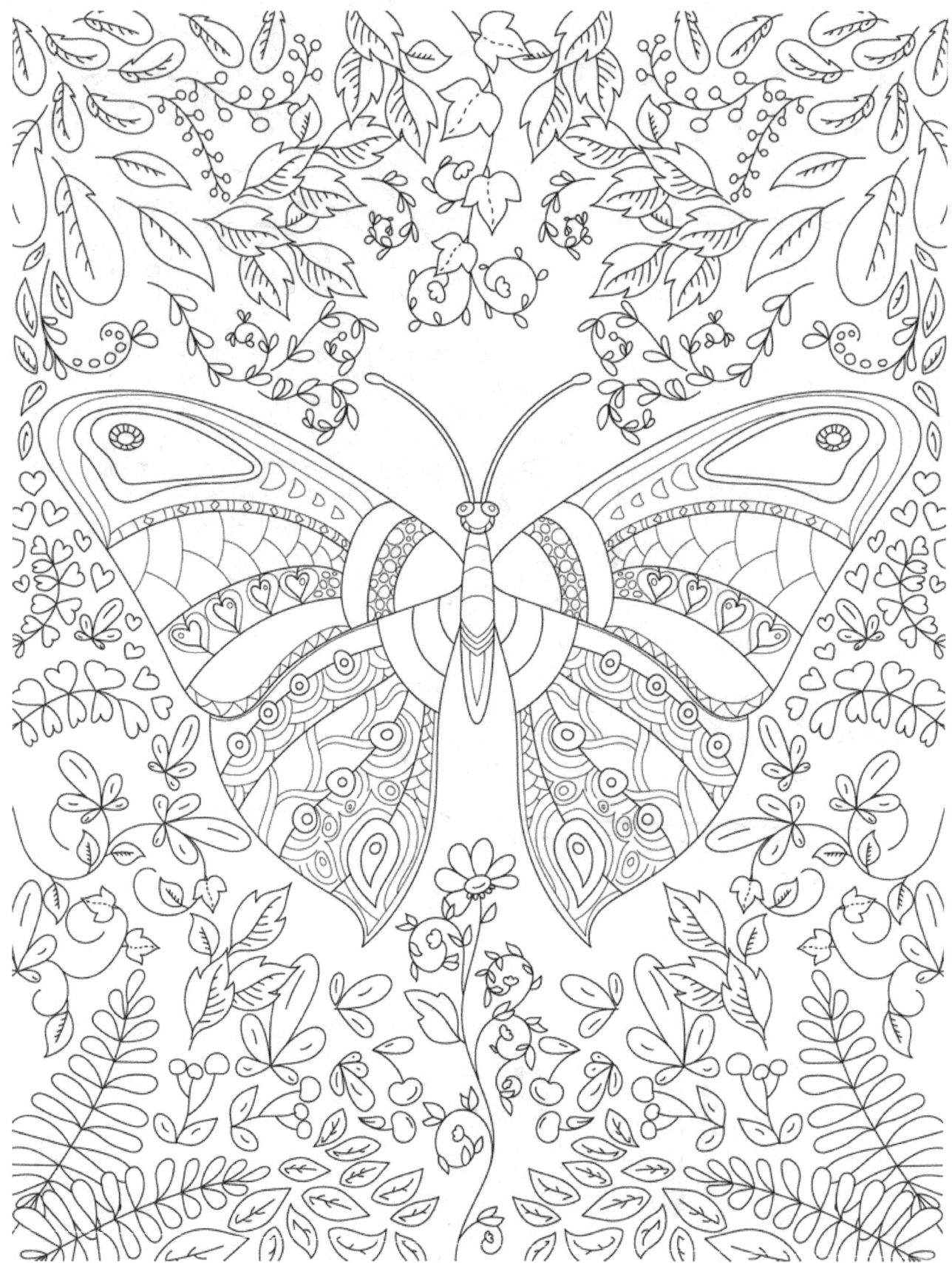

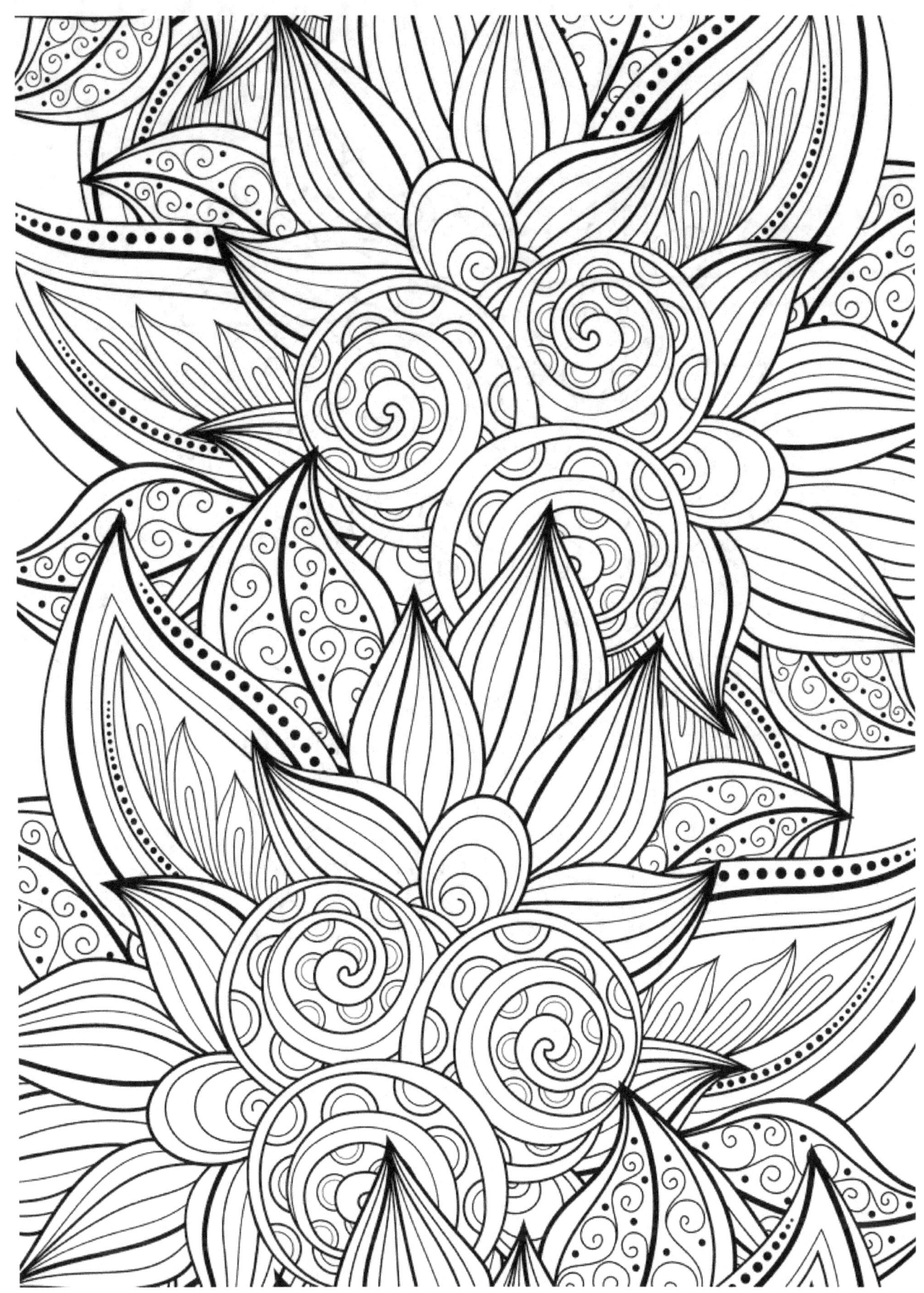

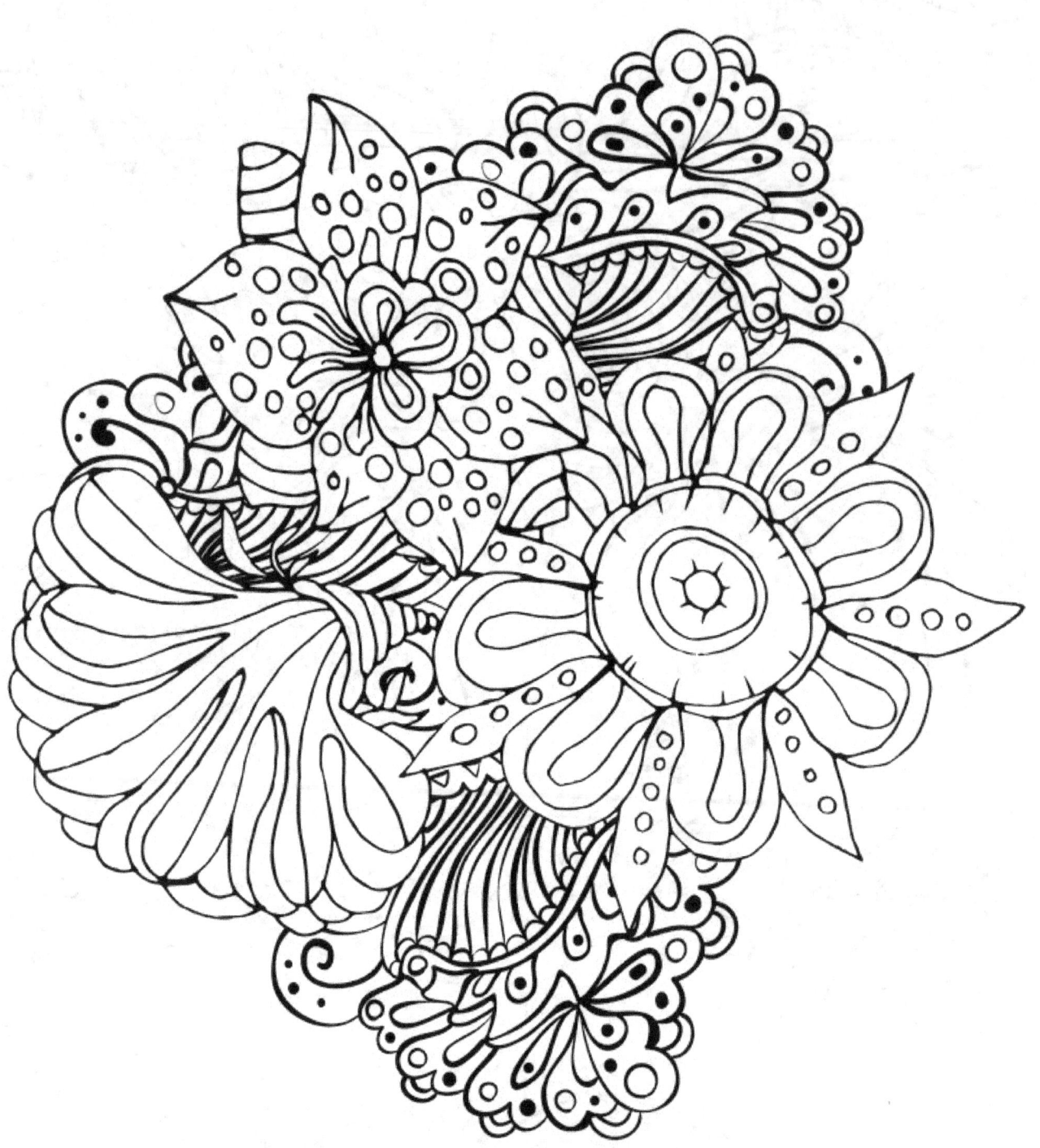

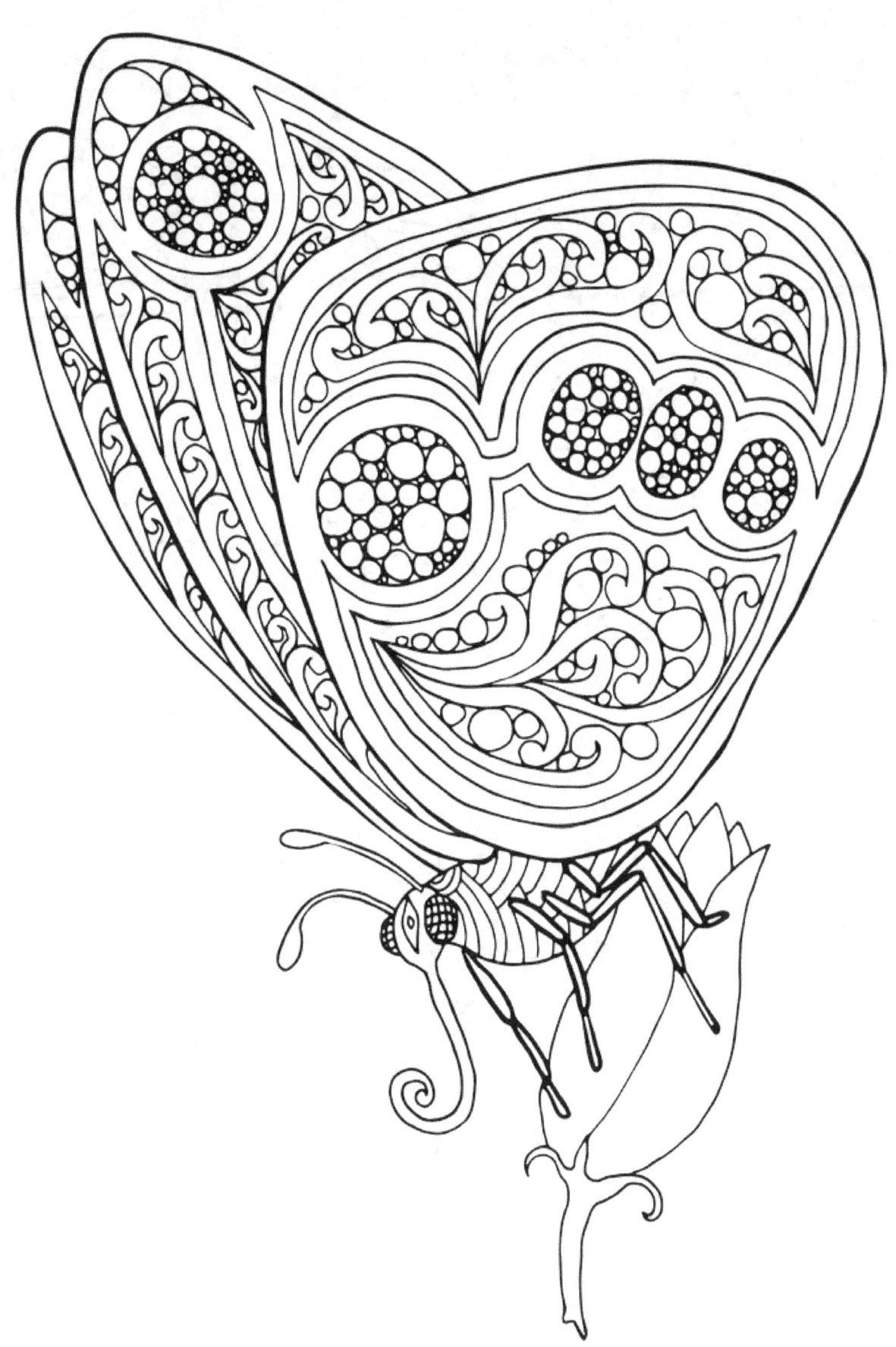

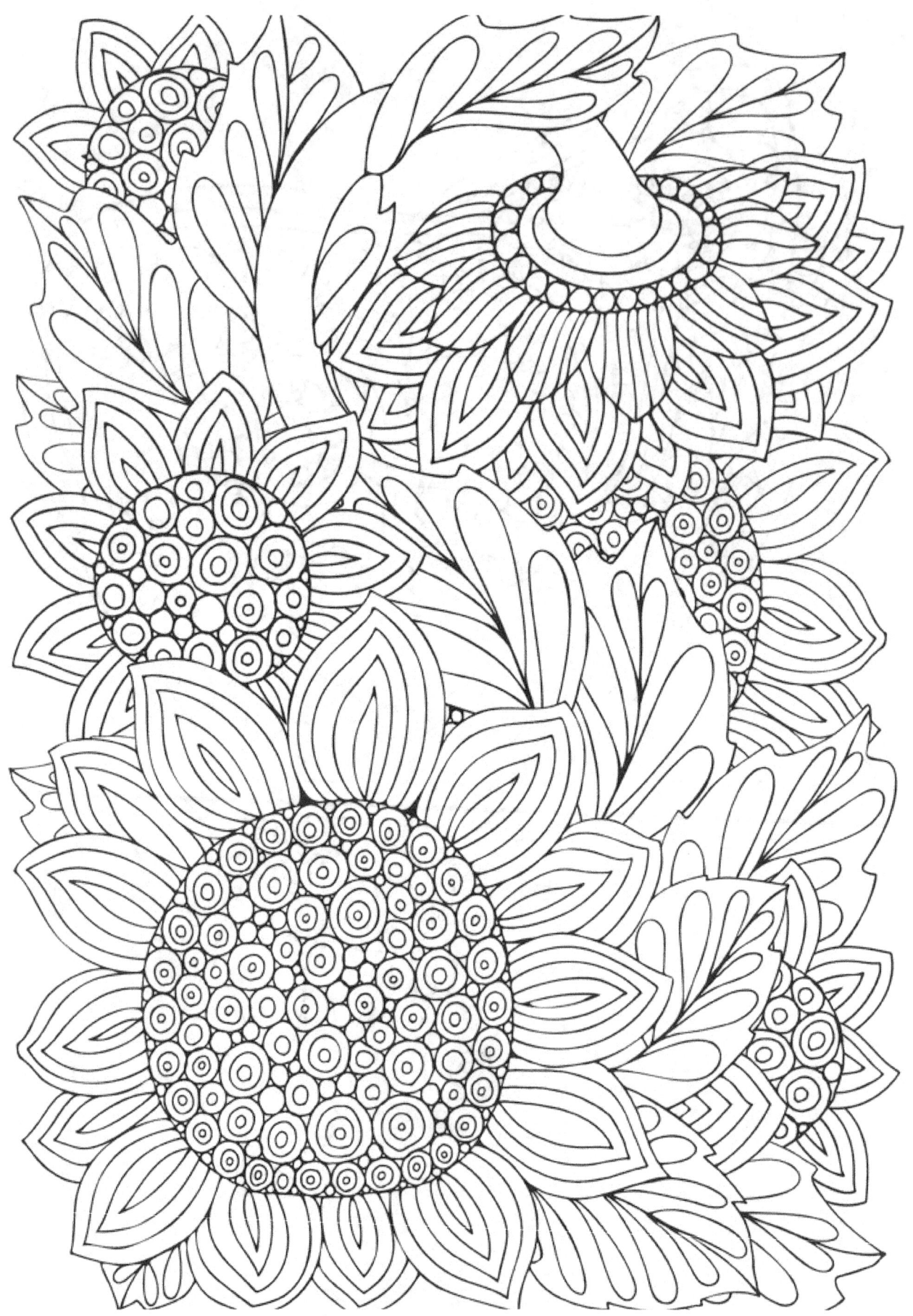

IF YOU LIKED THIS BOOK THEN WE RECOMMEND THAT YOU MIGHT LIKE THIS ONE TOO! PLEASE SCAN THE CODE BELOW:

FOR THE US

FOR THE UK

PLEASE TAKE A LOOK AT OUR OTHER COLORING BOOKS - PLEASE SCAN THE CODE BELOW

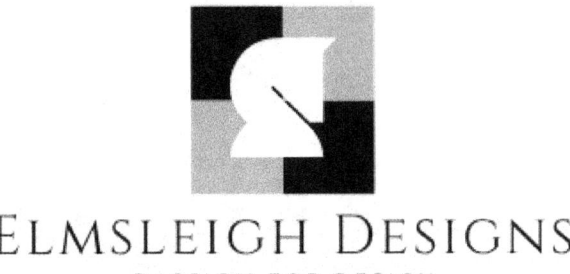

Elmsleigh Designs

PASSION FOR DESIGN